Advanced
Modular
Mathematics

MECHANICS 1

Graham Smithers

D1334915

SECOND
EDITION

COLLINS

nec
NATIONAL
EXTENSION
COLLEGE

Unit M1   T

Published by HarperCollins Publishers Limited
77–85 Fulham Palace Road
Hammersmith
London W6 8JB

www.CollinsEducation.com
On-line Support for Schools and Colleges

© National Extension College Trust Ltd 2000
First published 2000
ISBN 000 322515 1

This book was written by Graham Smithers for the National Extension College Trust Ltd.

British Library Cataloguing in Publication Data
A catalogue record for this publication is available from the British Library.

Original internal design: Derek Lee
Cover design and implementation: Terry Bambrook
Project editors: Hugh Hillyard-Parker and Margaret Levin
Page layout: Mary Bishop
Printed and bound: Martins the Printers Ltd., Berwick-upon-Tweed

The authors and publishers thank Dave Wilkins for his comments on this book.

The National Extension College is an educational trust and a registered charity with a distinguished body of trustees. It is an independent, self-financing organisation.

Since it was established in 1963, NEC has pioneered the development of flexible learning for adults. NEC is actively developing innovative materials and systems for distance-learning options from basic skills and general education to degree and professional training.

For further details of NEC resources that support Advanced Modular Mathematics, and other NEC courses, contact NEC Customer Services:

National Extension College Trust Ltd
18 Brooklands Avenue
Cambridge CB2 2HN
Telephone 01223 316644, Fax 01223 313586
Email resources@nec.ac.uk, Home page www.nec.ac.uk

You might also like to visit:

www.fireandwater.com
The book lover's website

M1
Contents

M1

Advanced Modular Mathematics

FOREWORD
This book is one of a series covering the Edexcel Advanced Subsidiary (AS) and Advanced GCE in Mathematics. It covers all the subject material for Mechanics 1 (Unit M1), examined from 2001 onwards.

While this series of text books has been structured to match the Edexcel specification, we hope that the informal style of the text and approach to important concepts will encourage other readers whose final exams are from other Boards to use the books for extra reading and practice. In particular, we have included references to the OCR syllabus (see below).

This book is meant to be *used*: read the text, study the worked examples and work through the Practice questions and Summary exercises, which will give you practice in the basic skills you need for maths at this level. Many exercises, and worked examples, are based on applications of the mathematics in this book. There are many books for advanced mathematics, which include many more exercises: use this book to direct your studies, making use of as many other resources as you can.

There are many features in this book that you will find particularly useful:

- Each **section** covers one discrete area of the new Edexcel specification. The order of topics is exactly the same as in the specification.

- **Practice questions** are given at regular intervals throughout each section. The questions are graded to help you build up your mathematical skills gradually through the section. The **Answers** to these questions come at the end of the relevant section.

- **Summary exercises** are given at the end of each section; these include more full-blown, exam-type questions. Full, worked solutions are given in a separate **Solutions** section at the end of the book.

- In addition, we have provided a complete **Practice examination paper**, which you can use as a 'dummy run' of the actual exam when you reach the end of your studies on M1.

- Alongside most of the headings in this book you will see boxed references, e.g. OCR **M1** 5.7.1 (a) These are for students following the OCR specification and indicate which part of that specification the topic covers.

- Key Skills: because of the nature of mechanics, your work on this book will not provide many obvious opportunities for gathering evidence of Key Skills, and so we have not included any Key Skills references (as we have done in other books in this series).

The National Extension College has more experience of flexible-learning materials than any other body (see p. ii). This series is a distillation of that experience: Advanced Modular Mathematics helps to put you in control of your own learning.

1

Mathematical models in mechanics

Certain *mathematical skills* are needed in your work throughout this module, and so this first section starts by:

- listing those particular mathematical skills that will be assumed in later sections

- looking especially at vectors, which can often provide a useful notation in mechanics.

Certain *mathematical terms* are also used in this module and therefore this section also:

- provides a glossary of these terms

- looks especially at how these terms are used in mathematical models.

Modelling is a way of describing real-life situations in terms of mathematical problems. Apart from being a useful way of approaching – and often simplifying problems – modelling often features as part of 'A' level examination questions.

Mathematical skills assumed $\boxed{\text{OCR M1}}$

You should be familiar with the following:

- solving the quadratic equation $ax^2 + bx + c = 0$ by means of the formula:

$$\frac{-b \pm \sqrt{b^2 - 4ac}}{2a}$$

- solving some equations by factors, e.g.

$$t^2 - 6t = 0 \Rightarrow t(t - 6) = 0 \Rightarrow t = 0 \text{ or } 6$$

- multiplying out brackets, e.g.

$$(t - 1)^2 + (2t - 3)^2 = 5t^2 - 14t + 10$$

- using factors, e.g.

$$R^2 - r^2 = (R - r)(R + r)$$

- the definitions and use of trigonometric functions:

$$\Rightarrow \sin x = \frac{O}{H}, \cos x = \frac{A}{H}, \tan x = \frac{O}{A}$$

- drawing a tangent to estimate the gradient of a curve at any particular point.

Practice questions A

1 Solve the equation $3x^2 + 4x - 5 = 0$.
Give your answers correct to 3 d.p.

2 Solve the equation $3x^2 - 4x = 0$.
Give your answers in exact form.

3 Simplify: $(2t + 1)^2 + (3t - 2)^2$.

4 Factorise:
(a) $x^2 - 9y^2$ (b) $2x^2 - 50$

5 Look at the right-angled triangle below:

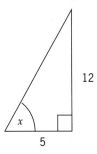

Find the exact value of:

(a) $\sin x$ (b) $\cos x$ (c) $\tan x$

6 Look at the right-angled triangle below:

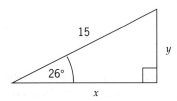

Find the values of x and y, giving each answer correct to 3 d.p.

7 Look at the right angled triangle below:

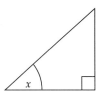

It is known that $\sin x = 0.96$. Find the exact value of $\cos x$.

8 Look at the graph below:

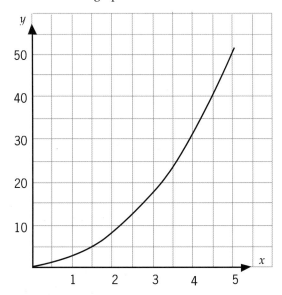

By drawing tangents, estimate the gradient of the curve when:
(a) $x = 2$ (b) $x = 4$

Vector notation

OCR M1

Figure 1.1 on the next page shows a grid with points A, B, C, D, E, F, G and H marked on it.

If we go from O to A, then we go 2 along the x-axis and 4 up the y-axis. We can write this as:

$$\overrightarrow{OA} = \begin{pmatrix} 2 \\ 4 \end{pmatrix}$$

Similarly we have $\overrightarrow{OB} = \begin{pmatrix} 8 \\ 2 \end{pmatrix}$ and $\overrightarrow{BH} = \begin{pmatrix} -4 \\ -5 \end{pmatrix}$

Figure 1.1

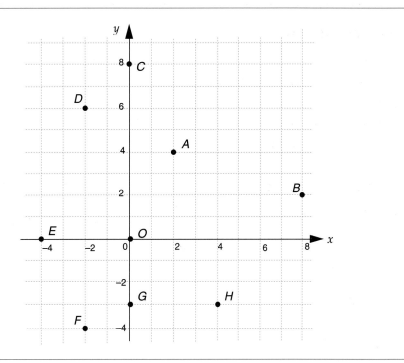

In general, if O is the origin and P has coordinates (x, y), then:

$$\overrightarrow{OP} = \begin{pmatrix} x \\ y \end{pmatrix}$$

It is conventional to call $\overrightarrow{OP}$ the position vector of P.

An alternative notation is to write:

$$\overrightarrow{OP} = x\mathbf{i} + y\mathbf{j}$$

where $\mathbf{i}$ indicates the direction of the positive x-axis and $\mathbf{j}$ the direction of the positive y-axis. In printed work, vectors are printed in bold type, as they are here; when writing them by hand, we put a line underneath $\underline{i}$ and $\underline{j}$.

Example

Referring to Fig. 1.1, obtain the vectors $\overrightarrow{ED}$ and $\overrightarrow{OG}$ in the form $x\mathbf{i} + y\mathbf{j}$.

Solution

$$\overrightarrow{ED} = \begin{pmatrix} 2 \\ 6 \end{pmatrix} \Rightarrow \overrightarrow{ED} = 2\mathbf{i} + 6\mathbf{j}$$

$$\overrightarrow{OG} = \begin{pmatrix} 0 \\ -3 \end{pmatrix} \Rightarrow \overrightarrow{OG} = 0\mathbf{i} - 3\mathbf{j} \Rightarrow \overrightarrow{OG} = -3\mathbf{j}$$

Example

Again referring to Fig. 1.1, if $\overrightarrow{CR} = 4\mathbf{i} - 11\mathbf{j}$, which of the marked points is R?

Solution

$$\overrightarrow{CR} = \begin{pmatrix} 4 \\ -11 \end{pmatrix}$$

∴ Beginning at C we go 4 along the x-axis and then 11 down the y-axis. But this means we finish up at H.

∴ R is the point H.

Example	P and Q have coordinates (1,3) and (5,12) respectively. Write down $\overrightarrow{PQ}$ and hence find PQ.

Solution	P to Q is 4 along the x-axis and 9 up the y-axis

$$\therefore \overrightarrow{PQ} = \begin{pmatrix} 4 \\ 9 \end{pmatrix}$$

The length of $\overrightarrow{PQ}$, usually called the *magnitude* of $\overrightarrow{PQ}$, is written as either $\mid \overrightarrow{PQ} \mid$ or, more simply, PQ and can be found using Pythagoras' theorem.

$$\therefore \overrightarrow{PQ} = \begin{pmatrix} 4 \\ 9 \end{pmatrix} \Rightarrow \qquad \Rightarrow \mid \overrightarrow{PQ} \mid = \sqrt{4^2 + 9^2} \Rightarrow PQ = \sqrt{97}$$

Example	If $\mathbf{a} = \begin{pmatrix} 2 \\ 3 \end{pmatrix}$ and $\mathbf{b} = \begin{pmatrix} 5 \\ -1 \end{pmatrix}$ find $3\mathbf{a} + \mathbf{b}$.

Deduce the magnitude of $3\mathbf{a} + \mathbf{b}$.

Solution	$3\mathbf{a} + \mathbf{b} = 3\begin{pmatrix} 2 \\ 3 \end{pmatrix} + \begin{pmatrix} 5 \\ -1 \end{pmatrix} = \begin{pmatrix} 6 \\ 9 \end{pmatrix} + \begin{pmatrix} 5 \\ -1 \end{pmatrix} = \begin{pmatrix} 11 \\ 8 \end{pmatrix}$

$\therefore$ magnitude of $3\mathbf{a} + \mathbf{b}$ (usually written as $\mid 3\mathbf{a} + \mathbf{b} \mid$) is given by:

$$\mid 3\mathbf{a} + \mathbf{b} \mid = \sqrt{11^2 + 8^2}$$
$$\Rightarrow \quad \mid 3\mathbf{a} + \mathbf{b} \mid = \sqrt{185}$$

Practice questions B

1   A, B and C have coordinates (2, 5), (3, 8) and (–4, 10) respectively. Write down the following:

   (a) $\overrightarrow{AB}$ (b) $\overrightarrow{AC}$ (c) $\overrightarrow{BC}$

   (d) $2\overrightarrow{BC}$ (e) $\overrightarrow{CA}$

2   If $\overrightarrow{PQ} = \begin{pmatrix} 8 \\ 15 \end{pmatrix}$ find PQ, the magnitude of $\overrightarrow{PQ}$.

3   If $\mathbf{a} = \begin{pmatrix} 6 \\ 2 \end{pmatrix}$ and $\mathbf{b} = \begin{pmatrix} 3 \\ -4 \end{pmatrix}$ find:
   (a) $\mathbf{a} + 2\mathbf{b}$ (b) $\mathbf{a} - 2\mathbf{b}$ (c) $2\mathbf{a} + \mathbf{b}$

   Deduce the magnitude of $\mathbf{a} + 2\mathbf{b}$, $\mathbf{a} - 2\mathbf{b}$ and $2\mathbf{a} + \mathbf{b}$.

4   If $\mathbf{a} = 2\mathbf{i} - 7\mathbf{j}$ and $\mathbf{b} = 7\mathbf{i} - 19\mathbf{j}$, find $\mathbf{b} - \mathbf{a}$. Deduce the magnitude of $\mathbf{b} - \mathbf{a}$.

5   If $\mathbf{a} = 6\mathbf{i} + y\mathbf{j}$ and $\mathbf{a}$ has magnitude 10, find *two* possible values for y.

6   If A, B and C have coordinates (–2, 3), (3, 5) and (7, 4) respectively, find the coordinates of P if $\overrightarrow{CP} = 3\overrightarrow{AB}$.

7   If $\mathbf{V} = \mathbf{U} + \mathbf{A}t$ where $\mathbf{V} = \begin{pmatrix} -3 \\ 13 \end{pmatrix}$, $\mathbf{U} = \begin{pmatrix} 3 \\ -2 \end{pmatrix}$ and $\mathbf{A} = \begin{pmatrix} 2 \\ -5 \end{pmatrix}$, find the value of t.

A glossary of mathematical terms

In your work on this module, you will meet all the following terms.

- A **particle** is a body possessing some mass but with dimensions small enough for it to be regarded as a single point. (In 'A' level questions, people are usually considered to be particles.)

- A **lamina** is a body which has mass and plane area but no thickness.

- A **rigid body** is one in which the distance between any two of its points remains constant.

- A **light rod** is a rod of negligible mass, i.e. it doesn't weigh anything.

- A **uniform rod** is a rod whose mass is symmetrically distributed about its centre. And so a uniform rod of mass 20 kg (say) can be regarded as a light rod with a particle of mass 20 kg attached to its centre.

- An **inextensible string** is a string which cannot be stretched.

- A **smooth surface** is a surface without friction.

Mathematical modelling

When solving a problem in mechanics, factors that have a negligible effect are often ignored. This has the advantage of simplifying the problem without sacrificing too much accuracy. This 'simplified problem' is called a *mathematical model* for the real situation.

Let's illustrate this with an example: suppose we have an object suspended from a fixed point by means of a piece of string.

- If it's a ball-bearing on the end of a piece of thick rope, then we would probably call the ball-bearing a *particle*.

- If it's a piece of cardboard on the end of the string, then we would probably say that *a lamina* was being suspended.

- If the object was an iron ball, then the weight of the string would be negligible compared to the weight of the ball. In that case we would probably say that we have a *rigid body* suspended by a *light string*.

- If the object is made to slide across a table top which has hardly any roughness in it, then we would probably say that the surface was *smooth*.

| Example | Anne has mass 50 kg and she is swinging on a plastic garden swing. What is a suitable model for this situation? |

| Figure 1.2 | 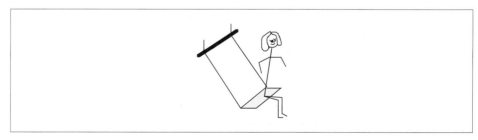 |

Solution	A particle of mass 50 kg suspended by a light inextensible string.
Figure 1.3	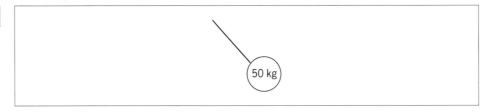

Example	Peter and John have masses 75 kg and 85 kg respectively. They are skating towards each other on an ice rink.
Figure 1.4	

What is a suitable model for this situation?

Solution	Two particles of mass 75 kg and 85 kg are sliding towards each other on a smooth surface.
Figure 1.5	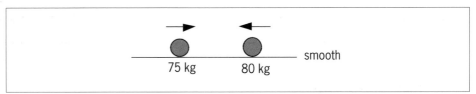

Example	A 20 kg ladder leans against a wall. Julia (70 kg) is standing three-quarters of the way up the ladder.
Figure 1.6	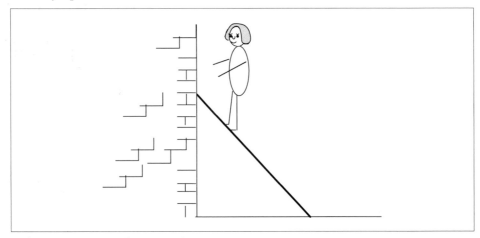

What is a suitable model for this situation?

Solution	A uniform rod of mass 20 kg is leaning against a vertical wall with its foot on horizontal ground. A particle of mass 70 kg is attached three-quarters of the way up.

Figure 1.7

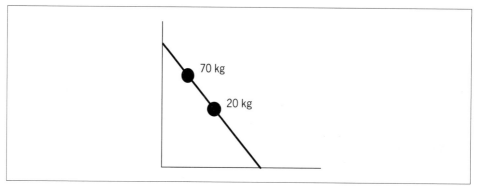

Practice questions C

1 What would be suitable models for the following:

(a) an unsharpened pencil   (b) a sharpened pencil   (c) a small sweet

(d) a bar of chocolate   (e) a sheet of paper   (f) a shoe lace

(g) an apple   (h) a hockey ball   (i) a bullet

(j) a pane of glass   (k) a needle   (l) a lap-top computer

(m) a biro   (n) a cube of sugar   (o) skin after applying face cream?

SUMMARY EXERCISE

1 Look at the grid below:

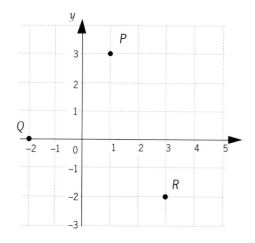

Express the following vectors in the form $x\mathbf{i} + y\mathbf{j}$:

(a) $\overrightarrow{OP}$ (b) $\overrightarrow{OQ}$ (c) $\overrightarrow{OR}$ (d) $\overrightarrow{RP}$ (e) $\overrightarrow{PR}$

2 If A and B have coordinates (2, 3) and (5, 10) respectively, find $\overrightarrow{AB}$ and $\overrightarrow{BA}$.

3 On the grid below, mark the points A, B and C where $\overrightarrow{OA} = \begin{pmatrix} 3 \\ 2 \end{pmatrix}$, $\overrightarrow{OB} = \begin{pmatrix} 1 \\ -3 \end{pmatrix}$ and $\overrightarrow{BC} = \begin{pmatrix} 4 \\ 3 \end{pmatrix}$

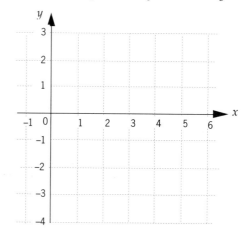

4   The position vectors of D and E are $3\mathbf{i} + 2\mathbf{j}$ and $7\mathbf{i} + 10\mathbf{j}$ respectively. Find the vector $\overrightarrow{DE}$.

5   If P and Q have coordinates $(3, 2)$ and $(5,7)$ respectively, find:

   (a) $\overrightarrow{PQ}$ (b) $|\overrightarrow{PQ}|$

6   Find the distance between the points P and Q whose coordinates are $(5, -2)$ and $(7, 4)$ respectively.

7   If $\mathbf{a} = \left(\begin{smallmatrix} 1 \\ -2 \end{smallmatrix}\right)$ and $\mathbf{b} = \left(\begin{smallmatrix} 3 \\ 4 \end{smallmatrix}\right)$, find $|\mathbf{a} + \mathbf{b}|$

8   What would be suitable models for the following:

   (a)   a motor car
   (b)   a door
   (c)   a drinking straw
   (d)   a lump of coal
   (e)   a piece of cotton
   (f)   a piece of elastic
   (g)   a plank of wood across a stream with a man standing on it
   (h)   an orange
   (i)   a bamboo cane
   (j)   a cricket ball flying through the air?

SUMMARY

In this section we have:

- used **vector notation**, e.g. if A has coordinates $(3, 5)$ then $\overrightarrow{OA} = \left(\begin{smallmatrix} 3 \\ 5 \end{smallmatrix}\right) = 3\mathbf{i} + 5\mathbf{j}$

- worked out the **magnitude of a vector**, e.g. if $\mathbf{a} = \left(\begin{smallmatrix} 3 \\ 4 \end{smallmatrix}\right)$, then $|\mathbf{a}| = \sqrt{3^2 + 4^2} = 5$

- used the following terms in order to **model real situations:**

particle	– a point mass
lamina	– a mass with area but no thickness
rigid body	– the distance between any two points of the body remains constant
light rod	– a rod of zero mass
uniform rod	– a rod whose mass is symmetrically distributed about its centre
inextensible string	– a string which cannot be stretched
smooth surface	– a surface without friction.

ANSWERS

Practice questions A

1 0.786 and –2.120

2 0 or $1\frac{1}{3}$

3 $13t^2 - 8t + 5$

4 (a) $(x - 3y)(x + 3y)$

(b) $2(x - 5)(x + 5)$

5 (a) $\frac{12}{13}$　　(b) $\frac{5}{13}$　　(c) 2.4

6 $x = 13.482,\ y = 6.576$

7

$\Rightarrow \cos x = 0.28$

8 (a) 8 (± 1)　　(b) 16 (± 2)

Practice questions B

1 (a) $\begin{pmatrix} 1 \\ 3 \end{pmatrix}$　　(b) $\begin{pmatrix} -6 \\ 5 \end{pmatrix}$　　(c) $\begin{pmatrix} -7 \\ 2 \end{pmatrix}$

(d) $\begin{pmatrix} -14 \\ 4 \end{pmatrix}$　　(e) $\begin{pmatrix} 6 \\ -5 \end{pmatrix}$

2 17

3 (a) $\begin{pmatrix} 12 \\ -6 \end{pmatrix}$　　(b) $\begin{pmatrix} 0 \\ 10 \end{pmatrix}$　　(c) $\begin{pmatrix} 15 \\ 0 \end{pmatrix}$

Magnitudes are $6\sqrt{5}$, 10 and 15.

4 $5\mathbf{i} - 12\mathbf{j}$. Magnitude = 13

5 $y = \pm 8$

6 (22, 10)

7 –3

Practice questions C

1 (a) uniform or light rod

(b) non-uniform rod or light rod

(c) particle

(d) lamina

(e) lamina

(f) inextensible string

(g) rigid body or particle

(h) rigid body or particle

(i) particle

(j) lamina

(k) light rod

(l) lamina or rigid body

(m) non-uniform rod or light rod

(n) particle or rigid body

(o) smooth surface

2

Kinematics of a particle moving in a straight line

You'll probably recall 'Damn Stupid Triangle', or as a means of remembering that: Distance = Speed × Time, Speed = $\frac{\text{Distance}}{\text{Time}}$ and Time = $\frac{\text{Distance}}{\text{Speed}}$. But *this only works if there is no acceleration*, i.e. it only works for constant speeds. And so what do we do if the speeds are variable?

In this section we'll attempt to answer this question by first looking at distance–time and velocity–time graphs, and what we can deduce from them. This will lead us to four useful equations connecting distance, velocity and (constant) acceleration. We'll then use these equations to model real situations such as a motor car accelerating along a level road or a stone falling vertically down a well.

The units for distance and displacement

OCR M1 5.7.3 (a)

Distance is usually measured in metres. For example, a distance of 8 metres is written 8 m.

If you look at the grid in Fig. 2.1, you'll see that P and Q are both 8 m from O.

Figure 2.1

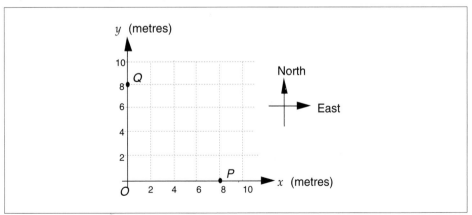

P and Q are the *same distance* from O but in *different places*. We say that the *displacement* of P from O is 8 m due East and the *displacement* of Q from O is 8 m due North. As you see, displacement is a distance together with a direction. In other words, displacement is a vector. And so:

Displacement of P from $O = \overrightarrow{OP} = 8\mathbf{i}$ (m) and *distance* $OP = 8$ m

Displacement of Q from $O = \overrightarrow{OQ} = 8\mathbf{j}$ (m) and *distance* $OQ = 8$ m.

11

The units for speed and velocity

Speed is usually measured in metres per second. For example, a speed of 12 metres per second is written 12 m/s or 12 m s^{-1}. Similarly 30 kilometres per hour may be written as either 30 km/h or 30 km h^{-1}. (Either notation is acceptable. In this module you will meet both forms of notation – this will help you become familiar with them both. In your own work you would be advised to choose the one you prefer and use that notation consistently.)

If you are driving along a straight road in a car at 20 m s^{-1}, then your speed is 20 m s^{-1}. If you then stop and start reversing at 2 m s^{-1}, then your speed becomes 2 m s^{-1}. But the directions of these speeds are different. In the first case we say that you have a velocity of +20 m s^{-1} and, in the second, a velocity of –2 m s^{-1}. And so **velocity** is a speed together with a direction. In other words, velocity is a vector.

The units for acceleration

Acceleration is usually measured in metres per second per second. And so an acceleration of 10 metres per second per second is written 10 m/s^2 or 10 m s^{-2}. Once again, either notation is acceptable and you need to be familiar with both of them.

Acceleration is another example of a vector. If you are gaining speed, then the acceleration is positive. If you are losing speed, then the acceleration is negative. Negative acceleration is sometimes called **deceleration** or **retardation**.

Practice questions A

1   Arabella is at point A(2, 5) and Benjamin is at point B (10, 20). [Distance measured in m.]

Write down the displacement $\overrightarrow{AB}$ and hence calculate the distance AB.

2   Convert a speed of 18 ms^{-1} to km h^{-1}.

3   Convert an acceleration of 5 m/s^2 to km/h^2.

4   The velocity **v** of a particle moving in a straight line is given by **v** = –5**i** m/s

(a)   What is the speed of the particle?

(b)   In which direction is the particle moving?

5   A particle P is accelerating parallel to the y-axis in a positive direction with an acceleration of 8 m s^{-2}. Write down the acceleration of P in vector form.

Distance–time graphs

Look at Fig. 2.2. What does this graph tell us? As you go from A to B, you cover 20 metres, then B to C another 20 metres and then 40 metres back to the start.

The distance from A to B is 20 m and this is covered in 4 seconds.

∴ Velocity while going from A to B is $\dfrac{20}{4} = 5$ m s^{-1}

But the gradient of AB also equals 5. And so:

> The gradient of a distance–time graph gives you the velocity.

Figure 2.2

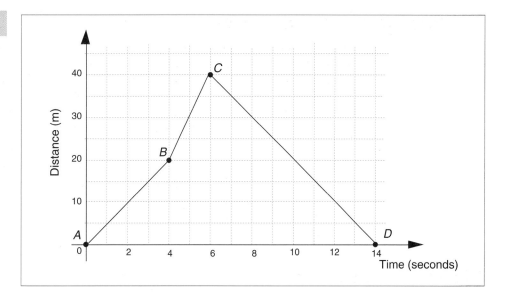

| Example | Look at Fig. 2.2. Find: |

(a) the velocity while going from B to C

(b) the velocity while going from C to D

(c) the velocity after 10 seconds

(d) the speed after 10 seconds.

| Solution |

(a) Gradient of $BC = \dfrac{20}{2} = 10$

∴ Velocity is 10 m s^{-1}.

(b) Gradient of $CD = \dfrac{-40}{8} = -5$

∴ Velocity is –5 m s^{-1}.

(c) Gradient at 10 seconds = gradient of line CD

∴ Velocity is –5 m s^{-1}.

(d) Speed after 10 seconds is 5 m s^{-1}.

| Example | A car moves away from a set of traffic lights. The distance-time graph shown in Fig. 2.3 describes the motion of this car during the first 5 seconds.

By drawing a tangent, estimate the speed of the car after 3 seconds.

| Solution | Begin by drawing a tangent, as best as you can, at the point $x = 3$. Do your best to ensure that your tangent only touches the curve at (3, 26).

Gradient of tangent $= \dfrac{12}{1} = 12$

∴ Speed of car approximately = 12 m s^{-1}.

Figure 2.3

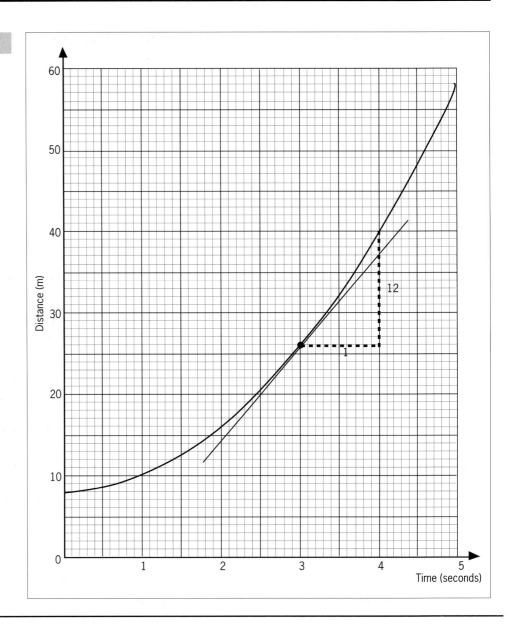

Practice questions B

1   Look at the distance–time graph below:

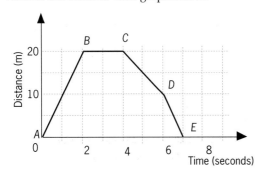

Find:

(a)   the velocity while going from *A* to *B*

(b)   the velocity while going from *B* to *C*

(c)   the velocity while going from *C* to *D*

(d)   the velocity while going from *D* to *E*

(e)   the total distance covered.

2 Look at the distance–time graph below:

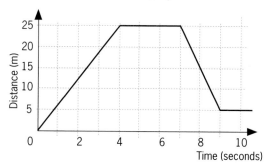

Find the velocity after:

(a) 3 seconds   (b) 5 seconds

(c) 8 seconds   (d) 10 seconds.

3

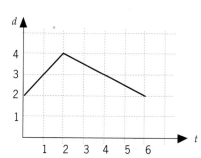

A snooker ball is moving in a straight line. Its displacement is d metres at time t seconds. The distance–time graph above describes its motion. Find the velocity of the snooker ball when:

(a) $t = 1$ (b) $t = 5$

Describe briefly what could have happened when $t = 2$.

4 The graph below illustrates a car journey from Halifax to York and back.

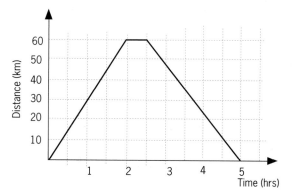

(a) How long does the journey to York take?

(b) What is the speed of this journey?

(c) What is the speed of the return journey?

5 The diagram shows the distance–time graph of a particle.

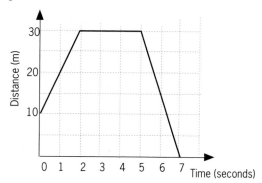

(a) Find the speed of the particle after 1 second.

(b) Find the average speed for the first 5 seconds.

6 The displacement d (in m) of a particle at time t (in seconds) is given by:

$$\mathbf{d} = \begin{cases} 4t \text{ i m} & \text{for } 0 \le t < 3 \text{ seconds} \\ 12 \text{ i m} & \text{for } 3 \text{ seconds} \le t < 5 \text{ seconds} \\ (22-2t) \text{ i m} & \text{for } 5 \text{ seconds} \le t \le 8 \text{ seconds} \end{cases}$$

Represent this information with a distance–time graph. Find:

(a) the total distance covered during the 8 seconds

(b) the velocity after:
  (i)   2 seconds   (ii) 4 seconds
  (iii) 7 seconds

(c) Describe briefly what happens when:
  (i) $t = 3$ (ii) $t = 5$.

7 Look at the distance–time graph below:

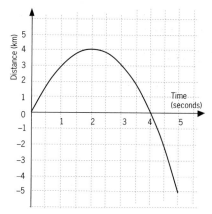

(a) What is the total distance travelled?

(b) What is the average speed?

(c) By drawing tangents, estimate the velocity after (i) 1 second (ii) 4.5 seconds.

8 A stone is dropped down a well.
Its displacement **d** (in m) at time t (in seconds) is given by:

$$\mathbf{d} = \begin{cases} -5t^2\mathbf{j}\,\text{m} & \text{for } 0 \le t < 4 \text{ seconds} \\ -80\mathbf{j}\,\text{m} & \text{for } t \ge 4 \text{ seconds} \end{cases}$$

(a) How deep is the well?

(b) Complete the following table:

Time (sec)	0	0.5	1	1.5	2	2.5	3	3.5	4
Displacement (m)	0	−1.25		−11.25					

Draw the corresponding displacement–time graph below:

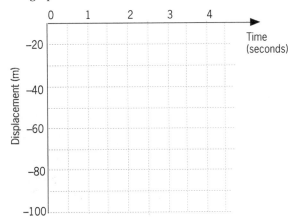

(c) By drawing a tangent, estimate the speed of the stone after 2 seconds.

9

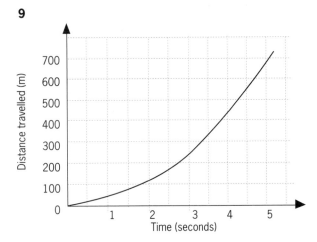

The distance travelled by a rocket, during the first 5 seconds after lift-off, is given by the graph above.

(a) What is the distance of the rocket from the launch pad after 4 seconds?

(b) By drawing a tangent, estimate the rocket's speed after 3 seconds.

(c) What is the average speed of the rocket during the 4th second?

10 A goods train moved slowly from rest to a signal at red. The table shows the distance from the starting point at various times.

Time (sec)	0	60	120	180	240	300
Displacement (m)	0	20	120	420	680	740

Draw the distance-time graph using 2 cm to represent 60 seconds and 200 metres.

(a) By drawing tangents, estimate the speed at:

(i) 120 seconds   (ii) 240 seconds

(b) By drawing a suitable tangent, estimate the greatest speed and the time at which this was reached.

Velocity–time graphs

OCR M1 5.7.3 (i),(iii)

Look at Fig. 2.4. What does this graph tell us?

As you go from P to Q, you get steadily faster until you reach a velocity of 10 metres per second. Then you cruise at this velocity for 2 seconds. Then, off you go again, steadily getting faster until, 4 seconds later, you reach a velocity of 20 metres per second. Finally, you gradually slow down until, after another 4 seconds, you come to a complete stop.

Figure 2.4

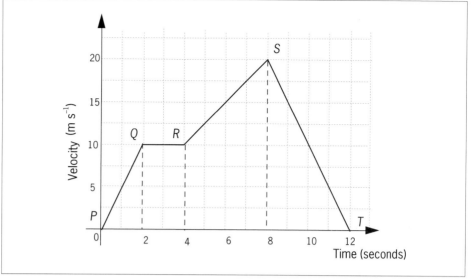

From P to Q you are getting faster. The acceleration is $\frac{10}{2} = 5$ m s^{-2}.

From Q to R you are going at a constant velocity of 10 m s^{-1}.

$\therefore$ You have no acceleration. And so:

> The gradient of a velocity–time graph gives you the acceleration.

But we can get more from this graph. Since you travel from Q to R at a constant velocity of 10 m s^{-1} and since this journey takes 2 seconds, *the distance from Q to R is $10 \times 2 = 20$ m.*

But 20 is also *the area under QR*. And so:

> The area under a velocity–time graph gives you the distance covered.

Example

Look again at Fig. 2.4. Find:

(a) the acceleration between R and S

(b) the acceleration between S and T

(c) the velocity after: (i) 6 seconds (ii) 11 seconds

(d) the total distance travelled

(e) the average speed for the whole journey.

Solution

(a) Gradient of $RS = \frac{10}{4}$ $\therefore$ Acceleration $= 2.5$ m s^{-2}

(b) Gradient of $ST = \frac{-20}{4}$ $\therefore$ Acceleration $= -5$ m s^{-2} ($\therefore$ slowing down)

(c) (i) 15 m s^{-1} (ii) 5 m s^{-1} Read these carefully off the graph

(d) Look at Fig. 2.5 for the area calculations.

Figure 2.5

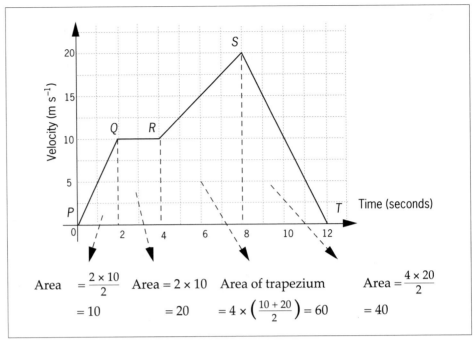

$$\therefore \text{ Total distance covered} = 10 + 20 + 60 + 40 = 130 \text{ m.}$$

(e)   Average speed $= \dfrac{\text{Total distance}}{\text{Total time}} = \dfrac{130}{12} = 10.8 \text{ m s}^{-1}$ (1 d.p.)

Example

A velocity–time graph is shown in Fig. 2.6.

Estimate the acceleration after 4 seconds.

Figure 2.6

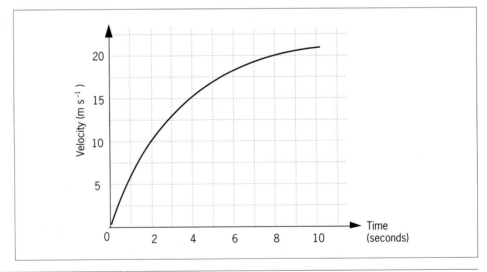

Solution

First of all we draw in the tangent at $t = 4$ seconds, doing our best to ensure that we draw in a line which only touches the curve at (4, 15) (see Fig. 2.7).

Gradient of tangent $= \dfrac{7.5}{4} = 1.875$.

$\therefore$ Acceleration after 4 seconds is approximately 1.875 m s^{-2}.

Figure 2.7

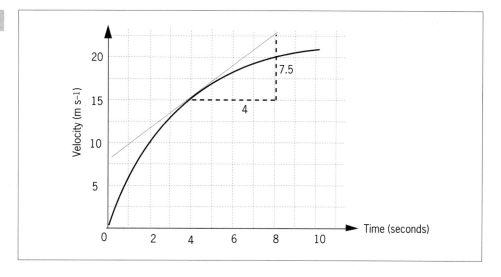

Example

A velocity–time graph is shown below. Estimate the distance covered during the first 8 seconds.

Figure 2.8

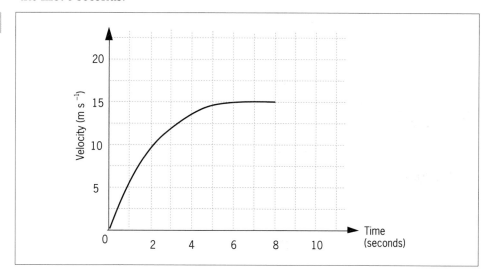

Solution

We need to estimate the area under the curve.

The usual way of doing this is to approximate the area as a sum of trapezia (see Fig. 2.9).

∴ Total area approximately = 10 + 23 + 28 + 30 = 91

∴ Total distance covered is approximately 91 m.

Figure 2.9

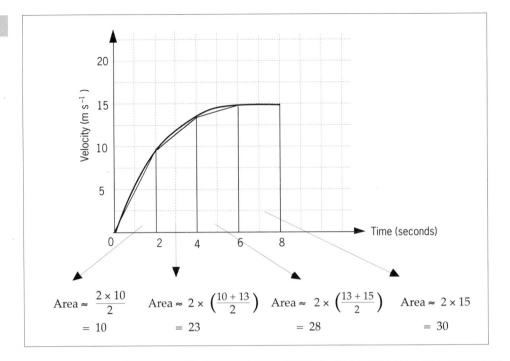

$$\text{Area} \approx \frac{2 \times 10}{2}$$
$$= 10$$

$$\text{Area} \approx 2 \times \left(\frac{10 + 13}{2}\right)$$
$$= 23$$

$$\text{Area} \approx 2 \times \left(\frac{13 + 15}{2}\right)$$
$$= 28$$

$$\text{Area} \approx 2 \times 15$$
$$= 30$$

Practice questions C

1 Look at the velocity–time graph below:

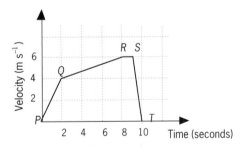

Find:

(a) the acceleration between P and Q

(b) the acceleration between Q and R

(c) the acceleration between R and S

(d) the acceleration between S and T

(e) the velocity after (i) 5 seconds (ii) $8\frac{1}{2}$ seconds

(f) the total distance travelled

(g) the average speed for the whole journey.

2

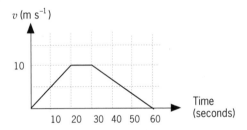

Consider the velocity–time graph above. Find the distance moved in 60 seconds.

3 The speed of a car is observed at regular intervals of time. The velocity–time graph shown below has been derived from these observations.

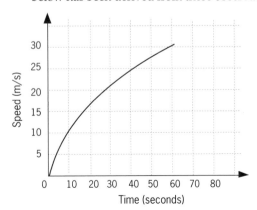

(a) By drawing a tangent, estimate the car's acceleration at $t = 20$.

(b) Use the graph to estimate how far the car travels in the first minute.

(c) At $t = 60$ the driver applies the brakes to produce a constant retardation of 2 m/s². Extend the graph to show this retardation and state the value of t when the car comes to a stop.

4 A rocket is fired and its velocity, v km/minute, t minutes after firing is given by

$$v = t^3$$

Complete the following table:

t	0	1	2	3	4
v	0		8		

Use scales of 2 cm ≡ 1 min and 1 cm ≡ 10 km/min to draw the velocity–time graph.

From your graph find:

(a) the acceleration 2 minutes after firing

(b) the velocity after $2\frac{1}{2}$ minutes

(c) the time when the velocity is 20 km/min

(d) the distance covered in the first 3 minutes

(e) the distance covered in the fourth minute.

5 The table shows the velocity, v m/s, of a helium filled balloon t seconds after being released in the air on a calm day.

t	0	1	2	3	4	5	6
v	0	5	8	9	8	5	0

Use scales of 1 cm ≡ 1 second and 1 cm ≡ 1 m/s to draw the velocity–time graph.

From your graph find:

(a) the maximum velocity of the balloon and when this occurs

(b) the velocity after $1\frac{1}{2}$ seconds

(c) the acceleration 1 second after release

(d) the acceleration when $t = 3$

(e) the distance covered by the balloon in these 6 seconds.

6

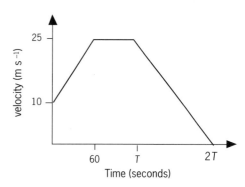

A train passes a signal box A with speed 10 m s⁻¹, and t seconds later its speed is v m s⁻¹ and its displacement from A is x metres. The velocity–time graph above models the train's journey from the time it passes A until it comes to rest at station B.

(a) Find the acceleration of the train when $t = 20$.

(b) Given that the average speed for the journey is 16.785 m s⁻¹, find T.

(c) Sketch the distance–time graph for the first 60 seconds after the train passes A.

7

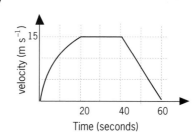

The velocity–time graph above represents a motor-cyclist travelling on a straight course.

(a) Calculate the distance travelled by the motor-cyclist as she was slowing down.

(b) Explain why the total distance covered is greater than 600 m.

(c) How would you estimate the acceleration after 10 seconds?

8

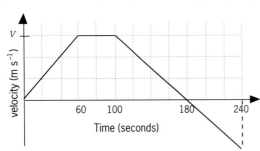

The velocity–time graph above represents a cyclist travelling along a straight road.

(a) Find an expression, in terms of V, for the distance travelled, in metres, by the cyclist in the first 180 seconds.

(b) If the average speed of the cyclist during the first 180 seconds is 5.5 m s^{-1}, what is the value of V?

(c) What is the cyclist doing immediately after 180 seconds?

(d) Find the distance of the cyclist from her starting point at the end of 240 seconds.

9

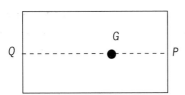

A golf ball G is projected towards point P with speed 4.5 m s^{-1}. It then rebounds and eventually comes to rest at Q.

The corresponding velocity–time graph is shown at the top of the next column.

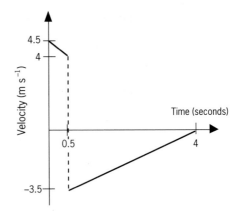

(a) Find the deceleration of the ball whilst travelling towards P.

(b) Find the distance from:
   (i) G to P (ii) P to Q.

(c) What assumptions have you made concerning the golf ball?

10 Consider the velocity–time graph below:

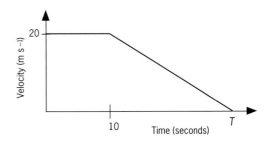

After 20 seconds the distance covered is 350 m.

Find: (a) the speed after 25 seconds
   (b) the value of T.

Acceleration–time graphs

Suppose a particle is moving in a straight line and its velocity–time graph is as shown in Fig. 2.10:

Figure 2.10

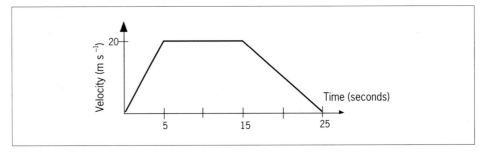

For the first stage of the motion, the acceleration of the particle $= \frac{20}{5} = 4$ m s^{-2}.

For the second stage, the particle is travelling at constant speed and so has zero acceleration.

For the third stage, the acceleration $= -\frac{20}{10} = -2$ m s^{-2}.

And so:

- the particle accelerates at 4 m s^{-2} for the first 5 seconds
- at 5 seconds, the acceleration suddenly becomes zero
- the particle has zero acceleration between 5 and 15 seconds
- at 15 seconds, the particle suddenly starts decelerating
- between 15 and 25 seconds, the acceleration of the particle is –2 m s^{-2}.

This can be represented graphically as follows:

Figure 2.11

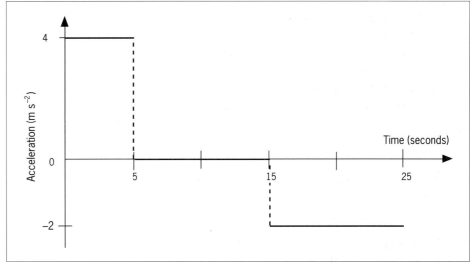

The above graph is the *acceleration–time* graph for the motion of the particle.

Practice questions D

1 Draw the acceleration–time graph that corresponds to the following velocity–time graph.

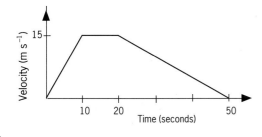

2 Draw the acceleration–time graph that corresponds to the following velocity–time graph.

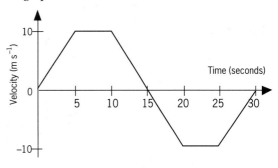

3 A particle is moving in a straight line and has the following acceleration–time graph.

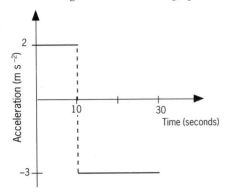

At time $t = 0$, the velocity of the particle is 6 m s^{-1}.

Draw the velocity–time graph for the particle for the first 30 seconds of its motion.

4 The velocity **v** (in m s^{-1}) at time t seconds of a particle moving in a straight line is given by:

$$\mathbf{v} = \begin{cases} 2t \, \mathbf{i} \text{ m s}^{-1} & \text{for } 0 \le t < 10 \\ 20 \, \mathbf{i} \text{ m s}^{-1} & \text{for } 10 \le t < 20 \\ (60 - 2t) \, \mathbf{i} \text{ m s}^{-1} & \text{for } 20 \le t \le 40 \end{cases}$$

Draw the corresponding velocity–time graph and acceleration–time graph. Hence complete the following for the acceleration vector **a**:

$$\mathbf{a} = \begin{cases} \ldots\ldots & \text{for } 0 \le t < 10 \\ \ldots\ldots & \text{for } 10 \le t < 20 \\ \ldots\ldots & \text{for } 20 \le t \le 40 \end{cases}$$

The usual symbols for displacement, velocity and acceleration

OCR M1

Mathematicians tend to use the same letters to represent certain things. For example, the quadratic equation is always written $ax^2 + bx + c = 0$. Very rarely do you see $\alpha f^2 + \beta f + \psi = 0$! Likewise in mechanics, certain letters stand for certain things. Let me list them for you:

s = displacement

t = time taken to cover that distance

u = initial velocity

v = final velocity

a = acceleration.

Generalising your earlier work

As we have just seen, the gradient of the velocity–time graph gives us the acceleration. Using this, together with the letters above, we get:

Figure 2.12

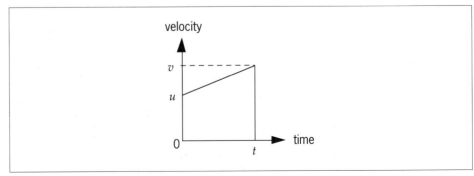

And since it's a straight line graph, we get a *constant* acceleration.

$$\therefore \quad \text{Gradient} = a = \frac{v-u}{t}$$

$$\Rightarrow at = v - u \Rightarrow v = u + at \qquad \qquad ①$$

But we have also seen that the area under the *velocity–time* graph gives us the distance covered.

$$\therefore \quad \text{Area} = s = t\left(\frac{u+v}{2}\right) \Rightarrow s = \left(\frac{u+v}{2}\right)t \qquad ②$$

Both equation ① and equation ② are very important. You will meet them constantly in your work on this module.

Example	Use the equations: $v = u + at$ and $s = \left(\frac{u+v}{2}\right)t$ to *deduce* the following:

(a) $\quad v^2 = u^2 + 2as$

(b) $\quad s = ut + \frac{1}{2}at^2$

(c) $\quad s = vt - \frac{1}{2}at^2$

Solution

(a) Equate the value of t from the given two equations:

$$\therefore \quad \frac{v-u}{a} = \frac{2s}{u+v} \Rightarrow (v-u)(v+u) = 2as \Rightarrow v^2 - u^2 = 2as$$

$$\Rightarrow v^2 = u^2 + 2as$$

(b) Substitute $v = u + at$ into the equation $s = \left(\frac{u+v}{2}\right)t$

$$\therefore s = \left(\frac{u+u+at}{2}\right)t \quad \Rightarrow s = \left(\frac{2u+at}{2}\right)t \quad \Rightarrow s = ut + \frac{1}{2}at^2$$

(c) Substitute $u = v - at$ into the equation $s = \left(\frac{u+v}{2}\right)t$

$$\therefore s = \left(\frac{v-at+v}{2}\right)t \quad \Rightarrow s = \left(\frac{2v-at}{2}\right)t \quad \Rightarrow s = vt - \frac{1}{2}at^2$$

Five constant acceleration equations

OCR M1 5.7.3 (d)

To sum up these results, you need to know and be able to use the following five equations:

$$v = u + at$$

$$s = \left(\frac{u+v}{2}\right)t$$

$$v^2 = u^2 + 2as$$

$$s = ut + \frac{1}{2}at^2$$

$$s = vt - \frac{1}{2}at^2$$

Let's look at some practical examples.

Example	A car accelerating uniformly in a straight line has speeds of 9 m s^{-1} and 24 m s^{-1} at times separated by 10 seconds. How far does it go during the period, and what is its acceleration?

Solution	Uniform acceleration $\Rightarrow$ constant acceleration

$\therefore$ We can use our four constant acceleration equations.

Let's begin by setting out the question systematically:

u	v	a	s	t
9	24	?	?	10

(We have been given u, v and t and have to find a and s.)

$\therefore s = \left(\dfrac{u+v}{2}\right)t \Rightarrow s = \left(\dfrac{9+24}{2}\right)10 \Rightarrow s = 165$ $\therefore$ Distance covered = 165 m

So now we have:

u	v	a	s	t
9	24	?	165	10

$\therefore v = u + at \Rightarrow 24 = 9 + 10a \Rightarrow 15 = 10a \Rightarrow a = 1.5$ $\therefore$ Acceleration is 1.5 m s^{-2}.

(We didn't use $s = 165$ this time, but it is always helpful if the table of results contains as much information as possible.)

Example	A train running at 16 m s^{-1} is brought to rest with constant retardation in $2\frac{1}{2}$ minutes. How far does it travel during this time and what is its retardation?

Solution	Constant retardation means that it is slowing down at a constant rate.

$\therefore$ We can use our four constant acceleration equations:

u	v	a	s	t
16	0	?	?	150

(change the $2\frac{1}{2}$ minutes to seconds first of all)

$\therefore s = \left(\dfrac{u+v}{2}\right)t \qquad \Rightarrow s = \left(\dfrac{16+0}{2}\right)50 \qquad \Rightarrow s = 1200$

$\therefore$ Distance covered = 1200 m or 1.2 km. And so:

u	v	a	s	t
16	0	?	1200	150

$\therefore v = u + at \Rightarrow 0 = 16 + 150a \Rightarrow -16 = 150a \Rightarrow a = -\dfrac{8}{75}$.

It is slowing down, and so the acceleration is negative.

The retardation is said to be $+\dfrac{8}{75}$ m s^{-2}.

Example	A skier increases her speed from 6 m s^{-1} to 18 m s^{-1} in a distance of 36 m. Find her acceleration.

Solution	

u	v	a	s	t
6	18	?	36	

$\therefore v^2 = u^2 + 2as \Rightarrow 18^2 = 6^2 + 72a \Rightarrow 288 = 72a \Rightarrow a = 4$

$\therefore$ Acceleration = 4 m s^{-2}.

Example	A stone is dropped down a well and gains speed at 9.8 m s^{-2}. It hits the bottom 3 seconds later. How deep is the well?

Solution

u	v	a	s	t
0	9.8	?		3

(It is dropped $\therefore u = 0$.)

$\therefore s = ut + \frac{1}{2}at^2 \Rightarrow s = 0 + 4.9 \times 9 \Rightarrow s = 44.1$ $\therefore$ The well is 44.1 m deep.

Example	A cyclist starts at 1 m s^{-1} and has an acceleration of 0.4 m s^{-2} for the first 100 m of his ride. How long does he take to travel this distance?

Solution

u	v	a	s	t
1		0.4	100	?

$\therefore s = ut + \frac{1}{2}at^2 \Rightarrow 100 = t + 0.2t^2 \Rightarrow 0.2t^2 + t - 100 = 0$.

And so now we have a quadratic equation to solve!

Using the formula $\dfrac{-b \pm \sqrt{b^2 - 4ac}}{2a}$ we get:

$t = \dfrac{-1 \pm \sqrt{1 + 80}}{0.4} \Rightarrow t = 20$ or -25

But we need a positive time. $\therefore$ Time taken is 20 seconds.

Example	Convert a speed of 18 km/h to m/s.

Solution

18 km/h   = 18000 metres in 3600 seconds

$= \dfrac{18000}{3600}$ m/s $= 5$ m/s

In mechanics, you'll often have to convert km/h to m/s. I find it very helpful to remember this conversion rule, i.e. 18 km/h = 5 m/s.

Example	*A* and *B* are two points, 100 m apart, on a straight road. A car, moving with constant acceleration along the road, takes 5 seconds to go from *A* to *B* and passes *B* with a speed of 25 m s^{-1}. What is the car's acceleration?

Solution

u	v	a	s	t
	25	?	100	5

$\therefore s = vt - \frac{1}{2}at^2 \Rightarrow 100 = 25 \times 5 - \frac{1}{2} \times a \times 5^2$

$\Rightarrow 100 = 125 - 12.5a$

$\Rightarrow 12.5a = 25 \Rightarrow a = 2$

$\therefore$ Acceleration is 2 m s^{-2}.

Practice questions E

1 A car is approaching traffic lights at 15 m s^{-1}, and the driver pulls up in 45 m. Find the deceleration, assumed constant, and the time taken to pull up.

2 An aeroplane takes off at a speed of 60 m s^{-1}, after accelerating uniformly from rest for 150 m. What is the acceleration, and how long is the aeroplane in taking off?

3 A particle starts with velocity 4 m s^{-1} and accelerates at 0.5 m s^{-2}. What is the velocity after 3 seconds and how far has it travelled during that time?

4 A particle is moving in a straight line and *decelerating* at 0.5 m s^{-2}. It passes point A with a speed of 20 m s^{-1}. Find its velocity after 10 seconds, the distance covered in that time and how much *further* the particle will go until it stops.

5 If a particle moving in a straight line passes a point P with speed 8 m s^{-1} and is accelerating at 5 m s^{-2}, how far will it travel in the next 6 seconds? How long will it take (from the start) to travel 602 m?

6 A motorist travelling at $u \text{ m s}^{-1}$ joins a straight motorway. On the motorway he travels with a constant acceleration of 0.05 m s^{-2} until his speed has increased by 2.8 m s^{-1}.

   (a) Calculate the time for this increase in speed

   (b) Given that the distance travelled while this increase takes place is 840 m, find u.

7 A particle has a constant acceleration of 6 m s^{-2} whilst travelling in a straight line between points A and B. It passes A at 2 m s^{-1} and B at 5 m s^{-1}. Calculate the distance AB.

8 A racing car starts from rest at the point A and moves in a straight line with constant acceleration for 30 seconds until it reaches point C. The speed of the car at C is 75 m s^{-1}.

   (a) Calculate the acceleration of the car.

   (b) If B is a point between A and C such that $AB = 245$ m, calculate the speed of the car as it passes B.

9 The points P, Q and R lie on a straight road such that $PQ = 50$ m and $QR = 100$ m. A cyclist, travelling with constant acceleration, passes P at 6 m s^{-1} and Q at 10 m s^{-1}.

   Find the speed of the cyclist at R, giving your answer correct to 1 d.p.

10 A sprinter runs a 100 metre race. She starts at 5 m s^{-1}, accelerates uniformly for 4 seconds to her top speed, and then maintains this top speed for the rest of the race. She covers the whole distance of 100 m in a total time of 11 seconds.

   (a) Sketch a speed–time graph to illustrate the motion of the sprinter during the time of the race.

   (b) Find her top speed.

11 The points O, A and B are in a straight line such that $OA = 40$ m and $OB = 210$ m. A motor car P, travelling along this line with constant acceleration, passes O at time 0 seconds, A at time 5 seconds and B at time 15 seconds. Find:

   (a) the acceleration of the car

   (b) the speed of the car at B.

12 O, A, B and C are points along a straight road. A car is travelling along the road in such a way that

   ● from O to A it increases its speed from 0 m s^{-1} to 6 m s^{-1} with a constant acceleration of $1.5a \text{ m s}^{-2}$

   ● from A to B it increases its speed from 6 m s^{-1} to 16 m s^{-1} with a constant acceleration of $1.25a \text{ m s}^{-2}$

   ● from B to C it increases its speed from 16 m s^{-1} to 36 m s^{-1} with a constant acceleration of $a \text{ m s}^{-2}$

   (a) Find, in terms of a, the total time taken

   (b) Given that the total time taken is 16 seconds, find the value of a

   (c) Find the total distance moved as the car accelerates from rest to 36 m s^{-1}.

Acceleration due to gravity

If you drop a stone over a cliff's edge, it will get faster and faster as it approaches the sea. This acceleration is caused by gravity. It is usually denoted by the letter g and, as far as your exam is concerned, is taken to be 9.8 m s^{-2}.

$$\therefore \text{ Acceleration due to gravity} = g = 9.8 \text{ m s}^{-2}.$$

In fact the acceleration due to gravity varies very slightly depending upon where you are. At the North Pole it is approximately 9.832 m s^{-2} whereas at Greenwich it is approximately 9.812 m s^{-2}. Then again, as you leave the earth's surface, the acceleration due to gravity decreases very slightly.

In taking g to be 9.8 m s^{-2}, what we are doing is making a mathematical model of the real situation. Since g varies only very slightly, taking it as having a constant value of 9.8 m s^{-2} will not affect significantly the validity of our results.

| **Example** | A marble falls off a shelf 1.5 m high. How long will it take to fall? |

Solution

$\downarrow$:	u	v	a	s	t
	0		9.8	1.5	?

(Falls off $\therefore u = 0$. I've added the arrow $\downarrow$ to indicate the direction of flight. You should find this helpful.)

$$\therefore \quad s = ut + \frac{1}{2}at^2 \Rightarrow 1.5 = 4.9t^2 \Rightarrow t = \sqrt{\frac{1.5}{4.9}} = 0.55 \text{ (2 d.p.)}$$

$\therefore$ The marble will take 0.55 seconds to fall.

| **Example** | An airgun pellet is fired vertically upwards at 49 m s^{-1}. How high does it rise? |

Solution

$\uparrow$:	u	v	a	s	t
	49	0	−9.8	?	

(It is travelling upwards so acceleration due to gravity is negative, i.e. −9.8 m s^{-2}; it reaches its highest point when $v = 0$.)

$$\therefore \quad v^2 = u^2 + 2as \Rightarrow 0 = 49^2 - 19.6s \Rightarrow s = \frac{49^2}{19.6} = 122.5$$

$\therefore$ The pellet rises 122.5 m

| **Example** | A ball is thrown vertically upwards at 8 m s^{-1} and caught at the same height. For how long is it in the air? |

Solution

First find the time to reach the highest point.

$\uparrow$:	u	v	a	s	t
	8	0	−9.8		?

$$\therefore \quad v = u + at \Rightarrow 0 = 8 - 9.8t \Rightarrow t = \frac{8}{9.8} = 0.816 \text{ (3 d.p.)}$$

The trick now is to say that *the time going up must equal the time coming down*.

∴   Total time = 2 × 0.816 = 1.63 seconds (2 d.p.)

And, incidentally, the speed with which it is caught again will be the same when it is coming down as its initial speed. ∴ It is caught at 8 m s^{-1}.

Remember these tricks – they are useful!

Example	A stone is catapulted vertically upwards at 29 m s^{-1}. For how long does its height exceed 34 m?

Solution	First find its time to reach 34 m.

∴   ↑: u v a s t

                    29   −9.8   34   ?

∴ $s = ut + \frac{1}{2}at^2$ ⇒ $34 = 29t - 4.9t^2$ ⇒ $4.9t^2 - 29t + 34 = 0$

Solve the quadratic and get $t = 1.16$ or 4.31.

But what can these *two* positive answers actually *mean*? The 1.61 seconds must be the time taken to reach a height of 34 m, and common sense says that the 4.31 seconds must be the time to fly up to its highest point and then back down to a height of 34 m.

∴   The time the stone is above 34 m = 4.31 − 1.61 = 2.7 seconds

Always be on the look out for these clever methods in mechanics – they save a lot of time!

Example	In the previous example, a stone was catapulted vertically upwards. What was the mathematical model? Write down some assumptions that were made.

Solutions	We modelled the stone as a particle. We assumed that the acceleration due to gravity remained constant and that there was no air resistance.

Practice questions F

(Take $g = 9.8$ m s^{-2}.)

1   A stone is let fall from the top of a building 20 m high. How long does it take to reach the ground and with what velocity does it strike the ground?

2   A stone is dropped from a bridge and reaches the ground in 1.5 seconds. How high is the bridge?

3   A man on the top of a tower of height 40 m holds his arm over the side of the tower and throws a stone vertically upwards with a speed of 12 m/s. Find the height above the ground of the highest point reached by the stone.

4   A stone is thrown vertically upwards from ground level with a velocity of 30 m/s. Find:

(a)   how long it is in the air

(b)   how high it rises.

5   A particle, thrown vertically upwards from ground level, reaches a height of 6 m. What was its initial velocity?

6   A cricket ball thrown vertically upwards from ground level takes 6 seconds to reach the ground again. How high does it rise?

7   A balloon which is stationary starts to rise with an acceleration of 2.5 m s^{-2}. What is the velocity 12 seconds later? If ballast is dropped at the end of 12 seconds, what will be the velocity of the ballast after another 12 seconds?

8 A fire hose delivers water vertically upwards with a velocity of 25 m s^{-1}. How high does the jet reach?

9 A ball is dropped from a height of 8 m onto a stone floor. If it rebounds with half the speed with which it hits the floor, find the height to which it rises after the rebound.

10 A stone is projected vertically upwards from ground level with a speed of 25 m s^{-1}. Find:

(a) the time taken to return to the ground
(b) the maximum height reached
(c) how long the stone was more than 30 m above the ground.

11 A stone is thrown vertically upwards from ground level at 30 m/s. Find:

(a) the height to which the stone rises
(b) the time to reach the greatest height
(c) the height of the stone after 2.5 seconds

(d) the times when the stone is at a height of 18 m
(e) the total time the stone is in the air
(f) the speed after 2 seconds.

12 A stone is thrown vertically upwards with a speed of 20 m s^{-1}. One second later a second stone is thrown vertically upwards with a speed of 25 m s^{-1}. At what height above the ground do they collide?

13 Two rockets are fired vertically from launching pads side by side. The first rocket moves vertically upwards with an acceleration of $7g$ and the second with an acceleration of $9g$. If the second rocket is fired 2 seconds after the first, find how long after its launching the second rocket overtakes the first.

14 A sandbag is dropped over the side of an observation balloon at a moment when it is ascending vertically at 4 m/s. The sandbag hits the ground 5 seconds later. How high was the balloon when the sandbag was dropped?

SUMMARY EXERCISE

1 Look at the graph below. Find:

(a) the velocity during the first 2 seconds
(b) the velocity after 5 seconds
(c) the velocity after 7 seconds.

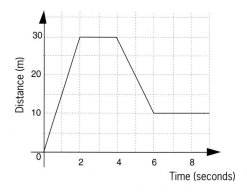

2 The graph below shows the distance of a train from London in km. Find the speed of the train in km h^{-1} at:

(a) 9:05 am   (b) 9:15 am

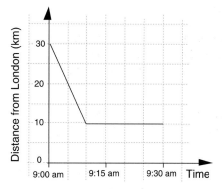

3 The graph below shows the velocity of a car.

(a) What is the acceleration for the first 4 seconds?

(b) What happens when $t = 4$?

(c) For how long is the car moving?

(d) For how long is the car braking?

(e) What is the total distance travelled?

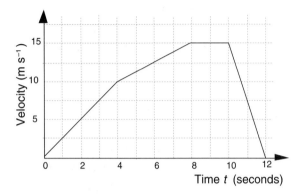

4 The figure below shows the velocity–time graph of a car journey between two sets of traffic lights.

(a) What is the acceleration of the car?

(b) What is the deceleration of the car?

(c) For how long does the car accelerate?

(d) How many metres does the car travel while braking?

(e) Find the distance between the two sets of lights.

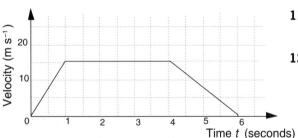

5 The following figure shows the velocity–time graph of a cross-country runner who covers three sections of the course in succession. The first is a downhill sweep, then there is a level section followed by a hill climb. Find:

(a) the acceleration of the runner on the downhill section

(b) the constant speed over the level section

(c) the deceleration of the runner during the hill climb

(d) the distance covered on the level section

(e) the distance covered on the hill climb.

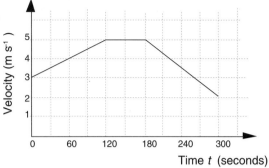

6 If a car is running along a straight road at 36 km h^{-1} and is stopped in 60 m, find the time taken to stop it.

7 If a train running at 48 km h^{-1} is stopped in 4 minutes, find the distance travelled before it is stopped.

8 A stone falling with an acceleration of 9.8 m s^{-2} starts from rest. Find its speed when it has travelled 40 m.

9 A car travelling with uniform acceleration clocks speeds of 7 m s^{-1} and 13 m s^{-1} at an interval of 3 seconds Find its acceleration.

10 A train accelerating at 0.1 m s^{-2} passes a signal box at 60 km h^{-1}. How far did it travel in the previous minute?

11 A coach travelling at 45 km h^{-1} pulls up in 100 m. What is the retardation in m s^{-2}?

12 The brakes of a train are able to produce a retardation of 1.5 m s^{-2}.

(a) In order to stop at the station, how far away must the driver apply the brakes if the train is travelling at 108 km h^{-1}?

(b) If the brakes are applied 27 m too late, with what speed will the train pass through the station?

13 A car accelerates uniformly in top gear from 14 m s^{-1} to 34 m s^{-1} in 20 seconds. Find:

(a) how far it travels while accelerating

(b) how long it takes to cover the first half of that distance.

14 (Skill required!) A cyclist reaches the top of a hill moving at 2 m s^{-1}, and accelerates uniformly so that, in the sixth second after reaching the top, he goes 13 m. Find his speed at the end of the sixth second.

15 A stone dropped from a bridge reaches the ground in 2 seconds. How high is the bridge?

16 A cricket ball thrown vertically upwards takes 5 seconds to reach the ground again. How high does it rise?

17 A balloon which is stationary starts to rise with an acceleration of 2 m s^{-2}. What is its velocity 10 seconds later?

If ballast is dropped at the end of 10 seconds, what will be the velocity of the ballast after another 10 seconds?

18 A fire hose delivers water vertically upwards with a velocity of 20 m s^{-1}. How high does the jet reach?

19 A ball is dropped from a height of 5 m on to a stone floor. If it rebounds with half the speed with which it hits the floor, find the height to which it rises after the rebound.

20 An aeroplane diving has an acceleration of 2g. What additional velocity does it acquire in 10 seconds?

21 A stone is dropped from the top of a cliff. A second later another stone is thrown downwards from the same point at 11 m s^{-1}. The two stones land at the same time. Find the height of the cliff.

22 A 100 m sprinter starts with a speed 6 m s^{-1}, accelerates uniformly to 10 m s^{-1} and finishes the race at this speed. Illustrate this information with a velocity–time graph.

If her total time is 10.4 seconds, find her uniform acceleration and after what distance she is going at full speed.

23 A car takes 2 minutes to travel between two sets of traffic lights 2145 m apart. It has uniform acceleration for 30 seconds, then uniform velocity, and uniform retardation for the last 15 seconds. Illustrate this information with a velocity–time graph and hence find the maximum velocity and its acceleration.

24 A particle is initially moving at 2 m s^{-1}. First it accelerates at 5 m s^{-2} for 3 seconds. Then it travels at a constant speed for the next 5 seconds. Finally, it decelerates at 2 m s^{-2} until it slows down to a speed of 1 m s^{-1}.

Illustrate this information with a velocity–time graph and hence find:

(a) the constant speed in the middle section
(b) the total distance covered.

25 A particle moving in a straight line with speed u m s^{-1} is retarded uniformly for 16 seconds so that its speed is reduced to $\frac{1}{4}u$ m s^{-1}.

It travels at this reduced constant speed for a further 16 seconds. The particle is then brought to rest by applying a constant retardation for a further 8 seconds. Draw a speed–time graph and hence, or otherwise:

(a) express both retardations in terms of u
(b) show that the total distance travelled over the two periods of retardation is 11 u m,
(c) find u given that the total distance travelled in the 40 seconds in which the speed is reduced from u m s^{-1} to zero is 45 m.

26 A particle A starts from the origin O with velocity u m s^{-1} and moves along the positive x-axis with constant acceleration f m s^{-2}, where $u > 0, f > 0$. Ten seconds later, another particle B starts from O with velocity u m s^{-1} and moves along the positive x-axis with acceleration $2f$ m s^{-2}. Find the time that elapses between the start of A's motion and the instant when B has the same velocity as A, and show that A will then have travelled twice as far as B.

27 Two particles P and Q move in the positive direction on the x-axis, P with constant acceleration 2 m s^{-2} and Q with constant acceleration of 1 m s^{-2}. At time $t = 0$, P is projected from the origin O with speed 1 m s^{-1}, and at time $t = 4$, Q is projected from O with speed 16 m s^{-1}. Find:

(a) the times between which Q is ahead of P
(a) the distance from O at which Q overtakes P
(a) the distance from O at which P overtakes Q.

28 A car starts from rest at time $t = 0$ seconds and moves with a uniform acceleration of magnitude 2.3 m s^{-2} along a straight horizontal road. After t seconds, when its speed is v m s^{-1}, it immediately stops accelerating and maintains this steady speed until it hits a brick wall when it comes instantly to rest. The car has then travelled a distance of 776.25 m in 30 seconds.

(a) Sketch a velocity–time graph to illustrate this information
(b) Write down an expression for v in terms of t
(c) Show that $t^2 - 60t + 675 = 0$.

SUMMARY	In this section we have seen that

- displacement is a distance together with a direction
- displacement is a vector
- the unit for distance is usually *m*
- velocity is a speed together with a direction
- velocity is a vector
- the units for speed are usually m s^{-1}
- acceleration is a vector
- the units for acceleration are usually m s^{-2}
- the gradient of a distance–time graph gives the velocity
- the gradient of a velocity–time graph gives the acceleration
- the area under a velocity–time graph gives the distance covered
- for constant (i.e. uniform) acceleration, the four relevant formulae are:

$$v = u + at$$
$$s = \left(\frac{u + v}{2}\right)t$$
$$v^2 = u^2 + 2as$$
$$s = ut + \frac{1}{2}at^2$$
$$s = vt - \frac{1}{2}at^2$$

where u = initial velocity
  v = final velocity
  a = (constant) acceleration
  s = displacement
  t = time taken to cover that distance

- the acceleration due to gravity is usually taken as 9.8 m s^{-2}.

ANSWERS

Practice questions A

1 $\binom{8}{15}$, 17 m

2 64.8 km h^{-1}

3 18 km/h^2

4 (a) 5 m/s

  (b) parallel to the *x*-axis in a negative direction

5 8**j** m s^{-2}

Practice questions B

1 (a) 10 m/s   (b) stationary $\therefore$ 0 m/s
  (c) –5 m/s   (d) –10 m/s   (e) 40 m

2 (a) $6\frac{1}{4}$ m/s   (b) stationary $\therefore$ 0 m/s
  (c) –10 m/s   (d) stationary $\therefore$ 0 m/s

3 (a) 1 m/s   (b) –0.5 m/s
  Probably hit the cushion and bounced off.

4 Missing values are 1, 27 and 64.
  (a) 2 hours   (b) 30 km/h (c) 24 km/h

5 (a) 10 m/s   (b) 4 m/s

6 (a)   18 m

(b)   (i) 4 m/s   (ii) at rest   (iii) –2 m/s

(c)   (i) suddenly stops   (ii) suddenly starts

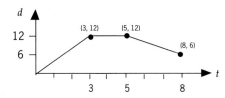

7 (a)   13 m

(b)   2.6 m/s

(c)   (i)   approximately 2 m/s

(ii)   approximately –5 m/s

8 (a)   80 m

(b)   missing values are: –5, –20, –31.25, –45, –61.25, –80

(c)   approximately 20 m/s

9 (a)   440 m

(b)   approximately 170 m/s

(c)   exactly 200 m/s $\left(\text{from} \dfrac{440 - 240}{1} \right)$

10 (a)   (i)   approximately 3 m/s

(ii)   approximately 1.7 m/s

(b)   approximately 6 m/s at 180 seconds.

Practice questions C

1 (a) 2 m/s^2

(b) $\frac{1}{3}$ m/s^2

(c) 0 m/s^2, steady speed

(d) -6 m/s^2

(e)   5 m/s and 6 m/s

(f)   43 m (4 + 30 + 6 + 3)

(g)   4.3 m/s

2   350 m

3 (a)   approximately 0.55 m/s^2

(b)   approximately 1145 m (using the trapezium rule)

(c)   75 seconds exactly

4 (a)   approximately 12 km/min

(b)   approximately 15.6 km/min

(c)   approximately 2.7 min

(d)   approximately 20.25 km

(e)   approximately 43.75 km

5 (a)   approximately 9 m/s at $t = 3$ seconds

(b)   approximately 7 m/s

(c)   approximately 3 m/s^2

(d)   exactly zero

(e)   approximately 35 m

6 (a) $\frac{1}{4}$ m s^{-2}

(b) $T = 120$ secs

(c)

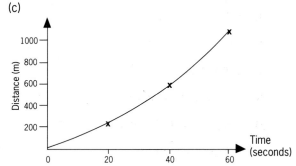

[Curve passes through (20, 250), (40, 600) and (60, 1050).]

7 (a)   150 m

(b)   Area of this trapezium

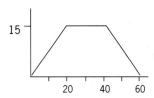

is 600 m.

Graph shown in the question has a greater area than this.

(c)   Draw a tangent to the curve when $t = 10$ seconds and calculate its gradient.

8 (a) $110V$

(b) $V = 9$ m s^{-1}

(c)   Returning home

(d)   787.5 m

9 (a)   Acceleration $= -1$ m s^{-2} (deceleration $= 1$ m s^{-2})

(b)   (a) 2.125 m   (b) 6.125 m

(c)   Assume the golf ball is a particle, i.e. negligible diameter

10 (a)   5 m s^{-1} (b) 30 secs

Practice questions D

1

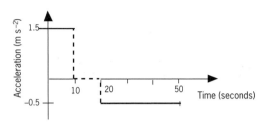

2

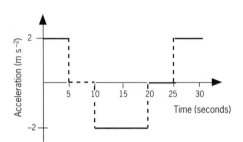

3

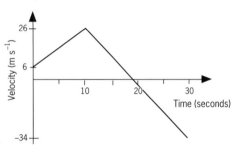

4

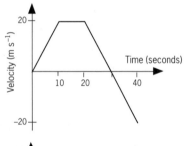

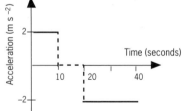

$$a = \begin{cases} 2\mathbf{i} \text{ m s}^{-2} & \text{for } 0 \leq t < 10 \\ 0 & \text{for } 10 \leq t < 20 \\ -2\mathbf{i} \text{ m s}^{-2} & \text{for } 20 \leq t \leq 40 \end{cases}$$

Practice questions E

1 $-2\frac{1}{2}$ m s^{-2}, 6 seconds

2 12 m s^{-2}, 5 seconds

3 5.5 m s^{-1}, 14.25 m

4 15 m s^{-1}, 175 m, 225 m

5 (a) 138 m (b) 14 seconds

6 (a) 56 secs (b) $u = 13.6$ m s^{-1}

7 1.75 m

8 (a) 2.5 m s^{-2} (b) 35 m s^{-1}

9 15.1 m s^{-1}

10 (a)

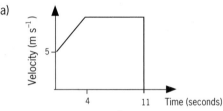

  (b) Top speed = 10 m s^{-1}

11 (a) 1.2 m s^{-2} (b) 23 m s^{-1}

12 (a) $\frac{32}{a}$ (b) 2 m s^{-2} (c) 310 m

Practice questions F

1 2.02 seconds, 19.8 m s^{-1}

2 11.025 m

3 47.35 m

4 (a) 6.12 seconds, (b) 45.92 m

5 10.84 m s^{-1}

6 44.1 m

7 30 m s^{-1}, 87.6 m s^{-1}

8 31.89 m

9 2 m

10 (a) 5.10 seconds (b) 31.89 m
   (c) 1.24 seconds

11 (a) 45.92 m (b) 3.06 seconds
   (c) 44.4 m
   (d) 0.674 seconds and 5.45 seconds
   (e) 6.12 seconds (f) 10.4 m s^{-1}

12 20.4 m

13 14.94 seconds

14 102.5 m

3

Dynamics of a particle moving in a straight line

INTRODUCTION   In the last section we looked at the basic principles of acceleration, and used the four constant acceleration equations to solve a number of problems. We'll now develop this theme by looking at the connection between force and acceleration.

When you have finished this section, you should be able to:

- distinguish between mass and weight
- work out the acceleration, given the force
- work out the force, given the acceleration
- solve problems involving connected particles
- work out momentum and impulse
- solve collision problems.

Mass and weight

OCR M1 5.7.2 (a)

My dog has a mass of about 12 kg but if he were on the moon, he would weigh much less – in fact, he would just be floating around. However, bring him back down to earth and all is well. His weight keeps him on the ground.

So his weight depends on gravity and the rule is:

Weight = mass × acceleration due to gravity

or $W = mg$, using standard symbols.

If we take $g = 9.8 \text{ m s}^{-2}$,

then the weight of my dog = $12 \times 9.8 = 117.6$ newtons or 117.6 N

Example	A brick has mass 1.5 kg. What is its weight?

Solution	Weight = $1.5 \times 9.8 = 14.7$ N

(Weight is always measured in newtons, provided that the mass is in kg.)

Force

Weight is an example of a force and so all forces are measured in newtons. The force necessary to push a bag of sugar along a table top would be something like 4 N. On the other hand, if you wanted to haul a load of bricks up on to some scaffolding, the force necessary might be in the region of 500 N.

Force and acceleration: the connection

Arminder and Bobby each have a trolley to push along a long, smoothly polished hospital corridor. Bobby's trolley is twice as loaded as Arminder's.

Figure 3.1

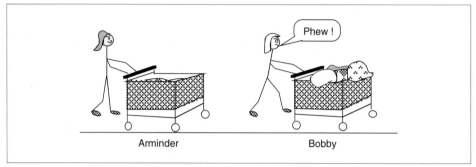

They both start to push their trolleys and wish to gain speed at the same rate. Who has to push the hardest? Clearly, Bobby. How much harder? Clearly, twice as hard. And so force must be proportional to mass.

Suppose now that Carla comes along and her trolley has the same load as Arminder's.

Figure 3.2

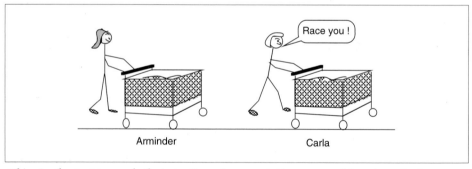

They both start to push their trolleys from a stationary position, but Carla pushes twice as hard as Arminder. What happens? Clearly Carla gains speed more rapidly – in fact, her acceleration will be twice as great. And so force must also be proportional to acceleration.

The rule is Force = mass × acceleration or $F = ma$, using standard symbols. It is known as Newton's Second Law.

> Newton's Second Law:
>
> Force = mass × acceleration

Example

An ice-yacht of mass 300 kg has an acceleration of 0.8 m s^{-2}. What force is needed to produce this?

| Solution | A diagram is always helpful in answering these sorts of questions: |

| Figure 3.3 | |

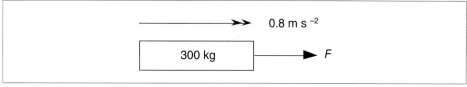

It is conventional to use double arrows for acceleration.

∴　$F = 300 \times 0.8 = 240$ ∴ force needed = 240 N.

| Example | A 6-tonne yacht is running before the wind. The wind produces a force of 350 N and the water a resistance of 50 N. Find the acceleration of the yacht. |

| Solution | Again, start by drawing a diagram: |

| Figure 3.4 | |

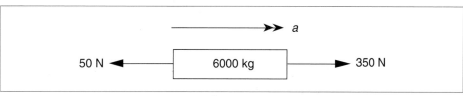

∴　$350 - 50 = 6000a \Rightarrow a = 0.05$ m s^{-2}

| Example | Six dogs pulling a 1500 kg sledge over level snow keep it going at constant speed. Eight dogs give it an acceleration of 0.3 m s^{-2}. With what force does each dog pull? |

| Solution | Let the force of each dog be D. |

| Figure 3.5 | |

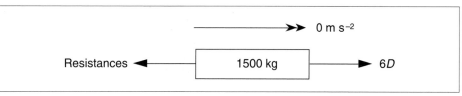

Steady speed $\Rightarrow$ no acceleration $\Rightarrow$ no overall force

∴　Resistances = $6D$.

With eight dogs we have:

| Figure 3.6 | |

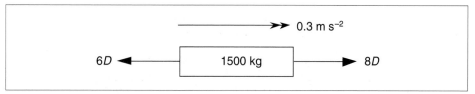

(The sledge will experience the same resistances, whatever the number of pulling dogs.)

∴　$8D - 6D = 1500 \times 0.3 \Rightarrow D = 225$

∴　Each dog has a pulling force of 225 N.

Practice questions A

1 A particle has mass 120 kg. What is its weight?

2 A particle has weight 49 N. What is its mass?

3

$\longrightarrow a$

50 kg	$\longrightarrow$ 200 N

(a) Find the acceleration a

(b) If it starts from rest, what is the speed after 12 seconds?

4

$\longrightarrow a$

160 N $\longleftarrow$ | 200 kg | $\longrightarrow$ 760 N

(a) Find the acceleration a

(b) If the initial speed is 3 m s^{-1}, what is its speed after 5 seconds?

5

$\longrightarrow$ 5 m s^{-2}

| 80 kg | $\longrightarrow$ F |

(a) Find the force F.

(b) If it is initially at rest, what distance is covered in the first 8 seconds?

6

$\longrightarrow$ 3 m s^{-2}

12 N $\longleftarrow$ | 20 kg | $\longrightarrow$ P

What is the force P?

7

$\longrightarrow a$

30 N $\longleftarrow$ | 70 kg | $\longrightarrow$ F

The 70 kg mass is moving at a steady speed.

(a) What is the acceleration a?

(b) What is the force F?

8

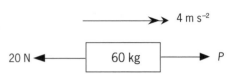

20 N $\longleftarrow$ | 60 kg | $\longrightarrow$ P, with 4 m s^{-2}

(a) What is the force P?

(b) When P is removed, what is the retardation?

9

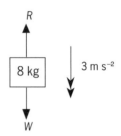

An 8 kg particle falls vertically downwards with acceleration 3 m s^{-2}.

The resistance to the motion is a force R and the weight of the particle is W.

(a) What is W in newtons?

(b) What is R in newtons?

10

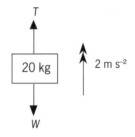

A 20 kg particle is hauled vertically upwards with acceleration 2 m s^{-2}. The 'hauling force' is T and the weight of the particle is W.

(a) What is W in newtons?

(b) What is T in newtons?

Initially the particle is at rest.

(c) What is the speed of the particle after 8 seconds?

Connected particles

OCR M1 5.7.4 (c)

These types of problem might involve a car pulling a caravan, or a train pulling a string of coaches, or a rope slung over a beam with weights at either end. The method is the same in all cases – you write down the separate equations (using $F = ma$) and then solve them.

But before we begin, we need to look a little more closely at the tension in a rope (or string). Suppose that two teams are entered in a tug-of-war and they are both pulling with a total force of 2000 N.

Figure 3.7

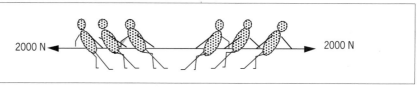

Clearly these teams are evenly matched and they are not going to move. Each team is being held back by the forces in the rope. Since both teams are pulling forwards with 2000 N, the force holding them back in the rope must also be 2000 N. And so the forces on the rope are:

Figure 3.8

∴ The tension at either end of the rope is the same (in this case, 2000 N).

In general, then, **if a rope is taut, the tension at either end will be the same**. Even if it is slung over a beam, providing the beam is smooth, the tensions at either end will still be the same.

Example

A car of mass 900 kg tows a caravan of mass 700 kg. If the driving force from the engine is 320 N, find the force transmitted through the towbar and the acceleration of the car.

Solution

Here, too, we start by drawing a diagram:

Figure 3.9

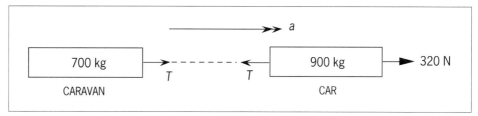

(Let T be the tension, the same at either end.)

Now use $F = ma$ on the car and caravan separately.

Caravan: $T = 700a$ ①

Car: $320 - T = 900a$ ②

Solve ① and ② simultaneously and get $T = 140$, $a = 0.2$

∴ The force is 140 N and the acceleration 0.2 m s^{-2}

When solving, it's nearly always easiest to just *add the equations*. In this case this gives us:

320 = 1600*a*, and so *a* = 0.2. Then substitution back gives *T*.

Example

A truck of mass 50 kg can run smoothly on horizontal rails. A light, inextensible rope is attached to the front of the truck, and this runs parallel to the rails until it passes over a light, smooth running pulley; the rest of the rope hangs down a vertical shaft, and carries a 10 kg load attached to the other end. Find the tension in the rope and the acceleration with which the truck and the load move. Comment on the modelling assumptions made.

Solution

A question written out like this sounds complicated. In examinations, however, you are likely to be given a diagram. Even if you are not, you can construct one of your own that models the situation.

And so we have:

Figure 3.10

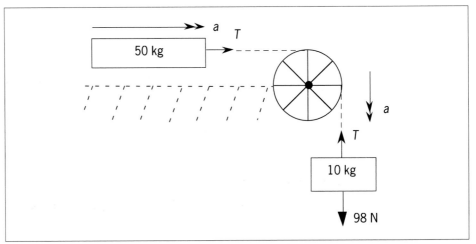

(The tensions, *T*, at either end of the rope are the same. The weight of the 10 kg load is 10 × 9.8 = 98 N.)

Truck: $T = 50a$ ①

Load: $98 - T = 10a$ ②

Now add ① and ② to get *a* = 1.63 (2 d.p.). ∴ Acceleration = 1.63 m s⁻²

Substitute back and get *T* = 81.7 (1 d.p.) ∴ Force = 81.7 N

As for the assumptions made, comments might include the following:

● The truck and load are assumed to be particles.

● There is assumed to be no air resistance.

● The acceleration due to gravity is taken as being constant.

● In real life a perfectly smooth surface would be impossible.

● We have assumed that the rope is weightless, although in reality it would be bound to have some mass.

| **Example** | Masses of 3 kg and 4 kg are joined by a string which is placed over a light, smoothly-running pulley so that one mass hangs vertically on either side. Find the acceleration with which the larger mass descends and the tension in the string. |

| **Solution** | Here is a diagram of this set-up: |

| **Figure 3.11** | |

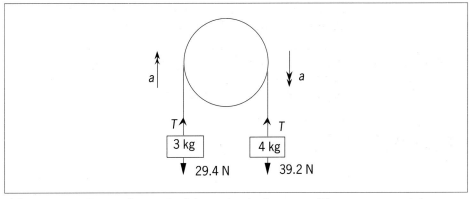

(The tension, T, at either end of the string is the same. The separate weights are: $4 \times 9.8 = 39.2$ N and $3 \times 9.8 = 29.4$ N.)

$$\therefore \quad 39.2 - T = 4a \quad \dots ①$$
$$T - 29.4 = 3a \quad \dots ②$$

Add and get $a = 1.4$

Substitute back and get $T = 33.6$

$\therefore$ The acceleration is 1.4 m s^{-2} and the tension is 33.6 N.

| **Example** | Masses of 39 kg and 10 kg are attached to the ends of a light inextensible string which passes over a smooth pulley. The 10 kg mass is held at floor level, and the other mass is 5 m above the floor. The system is released. |

(a)   After what time will the 39 kg mass hit the floor?

(b)   To what height will the 10 kg mass rise?

| **Solution** | (a) Initially we have: |

| **Figure 3.12** | |

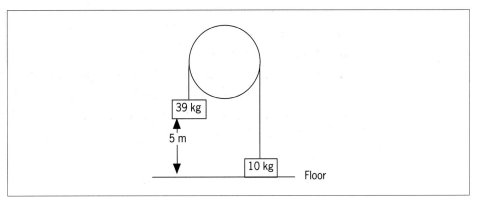

Subsequently we have the set-up shown in Fig. 3.13.

Figure 3.13

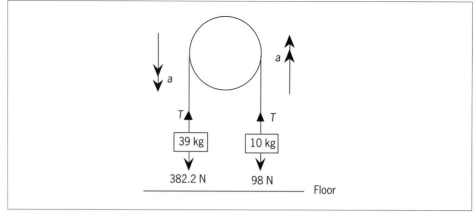

(The tension, T, at either end of the string is the same. The separate weights are $39 \times 9.8 = 382.2$ N and $10 \times 9.8 = 98$ N.)

$\therefore \quad 382.2 - T = 39a \quad ①$

$\qquad T - 98 = 10a \quad ②$

Add and get $a = 5.8$

$\therefore \quad ↓: \quad$

u	v	a	s	t
0		5.8	5	?

$\therefore \quad s = ut + \frac{1}{2}at^2 \;\Rightarrow\; 5 = \frac{1}{2} \times 5.8 \times t^2 \;\Rightarrow\; 5 = 2.9t^2 \;\Rightarrow\; t = 1.31$ (to 2 d.p.)

$\therefore \quad$ The 39 kg mass hits the floor after 1.31 seconds.

(b) We first need to find the velocity of the system just before the 39 kg mass reaches the floor.

$\therefore \quad ↓: \quad$

u	v	a	s	t
0	?	5.8	5	

$\therefore \quad v^2 = u^2 + 2as \;\Rightarrow\; v^2 = 2 \times 5.8 \times 5 \Rightarrow v = \sqrt{58}$ m s^{-1}

Once the 39 kg mass hits the floor, the string will go slack. The 10 kg mass, already 5 m above the floor and moving with an initial velocity of $\sqrt{58}$ m s^{-1}, will continue to rise but *this time, against gravity*.

$\therefore \quad ↑: \quad$

u	v	a	s	t
$\sqrt{58}$	0	-9.8	?	

$\therefore \quad v^2 = u^2 + 2as \;\Rightarrow\; 0 = 58 - 2 \times 9.8 \times s$

$\qquad\qquad\qquad\qquad\quad \Rightarrow 19.6s = 58 \;\Rightarrow\; s = 2.96$

$\therefore \quad$ The 10 kg mass will reach a height of $2.96 + 5 = 7.96$ m above the floor (before falling back down again).

Example

Two masses of 1 kg and 48 kg connected by an inextensible string 2 m long, lie on a smooth table 1.5 m high. The string is straight and perpendicular to the edge of the table. The lighter mass is drawn gently just over the edge and released. Find:

(a) the time that elapses before the first mass strikes the floor

(b) the time that elapses before the second mass reaches the edge of the table.

Solution

(a) Initially we have:

Figure 3.14

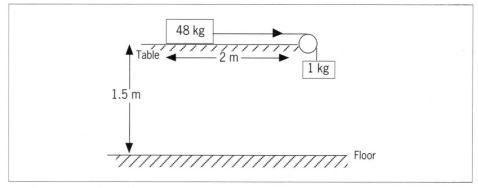

Subsequently we have:

Figure 3.15

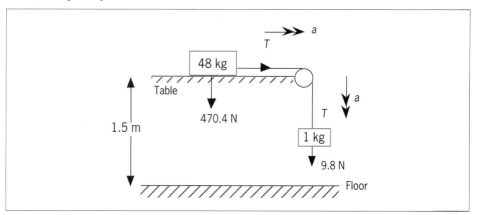

(The tension, T, at either end of the string is the same. The separate weights are $1 \times 9.8 = 9.8$ N and $48 \times 9.8 = 470.4$ N.)

$$\therefore \quad 9.8 - T = a \qquad \text{①}$$

$$T = 48a \qquad \text{②}$$

Add and get $a = 0.2$

$$\therefore \quad \downarrow: \quad \begin{array}{ccccc} u & v & a & s & t \\ 0 & & 0.2 & 1.5 & ? \end{array}$$

$$\therefore \quad s = ut + \frac{1}{2}at^2 \quad \Rightarrow 1.5 = \frac{1}{2} \times 0.2 \times t^2 \Rightarrow t = \sqrt{15}$$

$\therefore$ The first mass hits the floor after $\sqrt{15}$ seconds.

(b) We first need to find the velocity of the system just before the 1 kg mass hits the floor.

$$\therefore \quad \downarrow: \quad \begin{array}{ccccc} u & v & a & s & t \\ 0 & ? & 0.2 & 1.5 & \end{array}$$

$$\therefore \quad v^2 = u^2 + 2as \quad \Rightarrow v^2 = 2 \times 0.2 \times 1.5 \Rightarrow v = \sqrt{0.6} \text{ m s}^{-1}$$

Once the 1 kg mass hits the floor, the string will go slack. The 48 kg mass, now just $2 - 1.5 = 0.5$ m away from the edge of the table and moving with an initial velocity of $\sqrt{0.6}$ m s^{-1}, *will continue to move with that velocity*, because it will then be moving freely on a flat, smooth surface.

45

$\therefore$ Time taken to reach the edge of the table $= \dfrac{0.5}{\sqrt{0.6}} = 0.645$ seconds.

$\therefore$ The 48 kg mass will reach the edge of the table after a total time of $\sqrt{15} + 0.645 = 4.52$ seconds.

Practice questions B

1

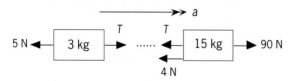

Find *a* and *T*.

2

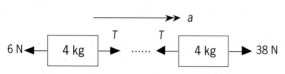

Find *a* and *T*.

3

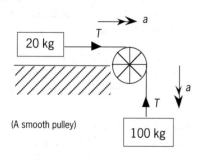

(A smooth pulley)

(a)   What is the weight of the hanging mass?

(b)   Find *a*

(c)   Find *T*

4

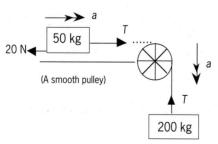

(A smooth pulley)

Find *a* and *T*.

5

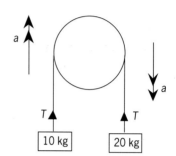

Find *a* and *T*.

6

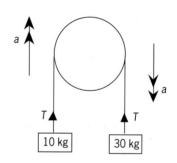

Find *a* and *T*.

7

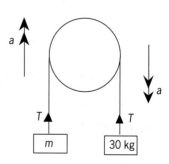

If $a = 4.2$ m s^{-2}, find the mass *m* and the tension *T*.

8

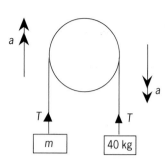

Find *m* and *T* in terms of *a* and *g* (gravity).

9

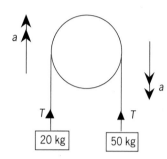

(a) Find *a* and *T*

(b) What is the force exerted on the pulley by the string?

10 A light inextensible string passes over a small fixed smooth pulley. The string carries a particle of mass 0.05 kg at one end and a particle of mass 0.02 kg at the other end. The particles move in a vertical plane, with both hanging parts of the string vertical. Find the magnitude of the acceleration of the particles and the tension in the string.

11 A 5 kg mass is connected by a thread which passes over a smooth peg to a 5 kg mass on top of which rests a disc of mass 5 kg, the masses hanging freely. Find the distance covered by each mass in 3 seconds after the system is released from rest and the tension in the thread.

If the disc is removed after 3 seconds, what further distance will each mass travel in the next 3 seconds?

12 Two masses of 7 kg and 9 kg, connected by an inextensible string 4.2 m long, lie on a smooth table 2.1 m high. The string being straight and perpendicular to the edge of the table, the lighter mass is drawn gently just over the edge and released. Find:

(a) the time that elapses before the first mass strikes the floor

(b) the time that elapses before the second mass reaches the edge of the table.

13 Two masses of 3 kg and 5 kg are connected by a light inextensible string passing over a smooth peg. Calculate the acceleration of the system. After moving for 2 seconds, the 5 kg mass strikes a table and does not rebound. Calculate the time for which it remains on the table.

14 Particles of mass 1.35 kg and 1.1 kg are connected by a string passing over a smooth pulley. With what acceleration does the greater mass descend?

After descending 4.5 m from rest, this mass is brought to rest again on reaching the ground. What further interval elapses before the string again becomes taut?

Momentum and impulse

OCR M1 5.7.5 (a)

If a mass *m* is subjected to a constant force *F*, its constant acceleration *a* is such that:

$$v = u + at \text{ and } F = ma.$$

Multiplying the first equation by *m* and then substituting for *ma*, we get:

$$mv = mu + Ft \text{ or } mv - mu = Ft \text{ ...①}$$

The quantity, mass × velocity, is called the *momentum* of the body. Its units are in newton-seconds or N s for short.

The quantity, force × time, is called the impulse of the force. Its units are also N s.

momentum = mass × velocity

impulse = force × time

impulse and momentum are measured in N s

∴ equation ① can be re-written as:

momentum after – momentum before = impulse

or

change of momentum = impulse

Example A 3 kg mass has a velocity of 5 m s^{-1}. What is its momentum?

Solution Momentum = 3 × 5 = 15 N s

Example A car of mass 1000 kg is pushed along a level road and acquires a speed of 2 m s^{-1} from rest in 10 seconds. What is the force pushing it?

Solution Using the change of momentum approach:

$$1000 \times 2 - 1000 \times 0 = 10F \quad \therefore \quad \text{The force} = 200 \text{ N}$$

(An alternative method would be to work out the acceleration first of all – it's 0.2 m s^{-2} – and then use $F = ma$. However, this change in momentum approach is much quicker.)

Example A hockey ball of mass 0.2 kg received an impulse of 1.2 N s at a free hit. With what speed does it begin to travel?

Solution $0.2\,v - 0.2 \times 0 = 1.2 \quad \therefore \quad v = 6 \quad \therefore$ Speed = 6 m s^{-1}

Example A hammer of mass 1.2 kg travelling at 15 m s^{-1} is brought to rest when it strikes a nail. What impulse acts on the hammer?

Solution $1.2 \times 0 - 1.2 \times 15 = \text{impulse} \quad \therefore$ Impulse = 18 N s

(The negative sign implies that the impulse is towards the hammer.)

Practice questions C

1 A 2 kg mass has velocity 4 m s^{-1}. What is its momentum?

2 A particle of mass 5 kg has a momentum of 45 N s. What is the velocity of the particle?

3 A saucer of 70 grammes is dropped from a height of 0.6 m. What impulse does it receive on striking the floor if it does not rebound?

4 A batsman receives a cricket ball of mass 150 grammes at a speed of 8 m s^{-1} and returns it straight back to the bowler at 12 m s^{-1}. What impulse does the bat give to the ball?

5 In what time will a force of 12 N reduce the speed of a particle of mass 4 kg from 18 m s^{-1} to 3 m s^{-1}?

6 A force of 20 N acts on a particle of mass 4 kg for 2 seconds. What is the increase in momentum?

7 A particle of putty, mass 0.6 kg, moving at 2 m s^{-1} hits a wall at right angles and stops dead. Find the impulse on the particle.

8 A hammer of mass 4 kg, travelling at 5 m s^{-1}, hits a nail directly and does not rebound. What is the impulse on the hammer? If contact lasts for 0.02 seconds, what is the average force between the two?

9 A tennis ball of mass 25 grammes travelling horizontally at 15 m s^{-1} is hit straight back at 35 m s^{-1}. If the impact lasted 0.02 seconds, what is the average force on the ball?

10 A horizontal jet of water is emitted from a circular pipe of radius 1.5 cm at a speed of 15 m s^{-1} and immediately hits a car. Find:

(a) the mass of water emitted each second

(b) the average force exerted on the vertical side of the car.

(Assume that 1 m^3 of water has mass 1000 kg.)

Collisions: conservation of momentum

OCR M1 5.7.5 (b)

Suppose that masses m_1, m_2 are sliding along a smooth table with speeds u_1, u_2. They collide and then move off with speeds v_1, v_2 respectively. If the impulse during impact is I, then:

Figure 3.16

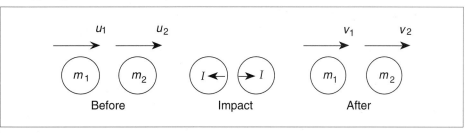

Taking each mass separately we get:

$$m_2 v_2 - m_2 u_2 = I \quad \dots \text{①} \qquad\qquad m_1 v_1 - m_1 u_1 = -I \quad \dots \text{②}$$

Now add ① and ② and get (after rearrangement):

$$m_1 v_1 + m_2 v_2 = m_1 u_1 + m_2 u_2$$

∴ the total momentum afterwards equals the total momentum before

That is the only rule you need in order to solve collision problems in Module M1.

Example

A railway truck of mass 1500 kg travelling at 5 m s^{-1} hits another truck of mass 1000 kg which is stationary. The two trucks couple automatically and go on together. With what speed do they move?

Solution

A diagram is always helpful:

Figure 3.17

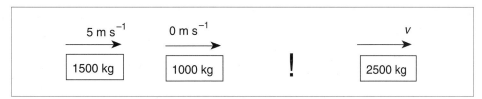

Conservation of momentum $\Rightarrow 1500 \times 5 + 1000 \times 0 = 2500 \times v \Rightarrow v = 3$

∴ Speed = 3 m s^{-1}

Example	A truck of mass 225 kg is moving at 3 m s⁻¹. A man of mass 75 kg runs straight towards it and meets it head-on at a speed of 6 m s⁻¹. If the man jumps on to the truck when he meets it, how fast and in what direction will the truck be moving afterwards?

Solution	Start with a diagram:

Figure 3.18

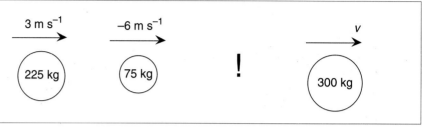

(Always get the speed arrows pointing in the same direction before you begin.)

$\therefore$ $225 \times 3 - 75 \times 6 = 300v \Rightarrow v = 0.75$

$\therefore$ Truck will move in the same direction at 0.75 m s⁻¹

Example	When a toy truck of mass 240 grammes hits another stationary truck mass 360 grammes its speed is reduced from 4 to 1 m s⁻¹. What speed is given to the second truck?

Solution	Again, start with a diagram:

Figure 3.19

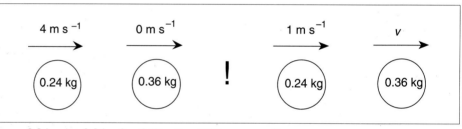

$\therefore$ $0.24 \times 4 + 0.36 \times 0 = 0.24 \times 1 + 0.36v \Rightarrow v = 2$

$\therefore$ The second toy truck gains a speed of 2 m s⁻¹

Example	A mass of $3m$ with velocity $4u$ strikes a mass of m moving with a velocity u in the same direction. If they coalesce, find their subsequent velocity in terms of u.

Solution	(Coalesce means 'join together'.)

Figure 3.20

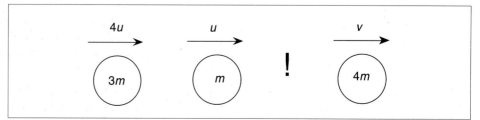

$\therefore$ $3\not{m} \times 4u + \not{m} \times u = 4\not{m} \times v$

$\therefore$ $12u + u = 4v \Rightarrow v = 3.25u$

Practice questions D

1 What is the total momentum of the system shown below?

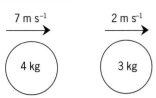

2 What is the total momentum of the system shown below?

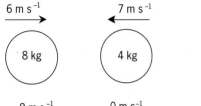

3

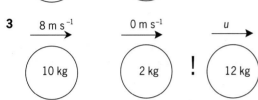

Find:

(a) u

(b) the impulse received by the 10 kg mass.

4

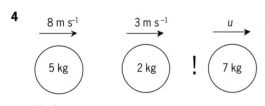

Find u.

5

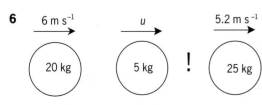

Find u.

6

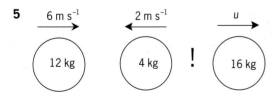

Find u.

7

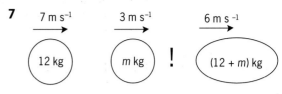

Find m.

8

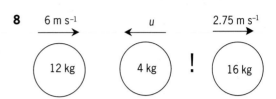

Find u.

9

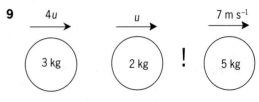

Find u.

10

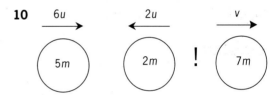

Find v in terms of u.

11 Particle A has mass 0.3 kg and particle B has mass 0.2 kg. The particles are travelling towards each other in the same line and they collide. Immediately before the collision the speed of A is 1.5 m s^{-1} and the speed of B is 3 m s^{-1}. Particle A is brought to rest by the collision. Find the speed of B immediately after the collision.

12 A marble A, of mass 0.03 kg, moving with speed 8 m s^{-1} in a straight line on a horizontal floor, collides directly with another marble B, of the same size as A and of mass 0.04 kg, moving with speed 5 m s^{-1} in the same direction. Immediately after the collision A and B continue to move in the same direction and the speed of A is reduced to 4 m s^{-1}. Find:

(a) the speed of B immediately after the collision

(b) the magnitude of the impulse exerted on A by B in the collision.

SUMMARY EXERCISE

1

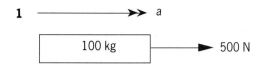

(a) Find acceleration a.

(b) If it starts from rest, what is its speed after 4 seconds?

2

(a) Find acceleration a.

(b) If the initial speed is 4 m s^{-1}, what is its speed after 3 seconds?

3

(a) Find force F.

(b) If it is initially at rest, what distance is covered in the first 4 seconds?

4

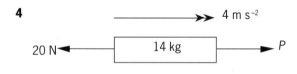

What is force P?

5

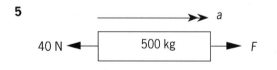

Moving at a steady speed:

(a) What is a?

(b) What is F?

6

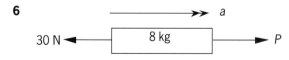

Moving at a steady speed:

(a) What is a?

(b) What is P?

(c) If P is suddenly removed, what is the retardation?

7

(a) What is F?

(b) When F is removed, what is the retardation?

8

Pull of the engine is F and resistances to motion are 20 N.

Initially the body is at rest. Force $F = 120$ N is applied for 6 seconds and then removed. How long will it be before the speed gets back to 2 m s^{-1}? (Talent required for this question!)

9

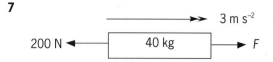

Pull of engine is F and resistances to motion are 80 N. Initially the body is at rest. Force $F = 120$ N is applied for 10 seconds and then removed. How long before it is back to rest and what will be the total distance covered?

10 A 400 tonne train crashes into the buffers at 18 km h^{-1} and depresses them 1.25 m, before coming to rest. What is the force of impact of the train on the buffers?

11 A brick of mass 3 kg falls through water with an acceleration of 2 m s^{-2}. Find the resistance force.

12 A 2-tonne lorry is being lowered into the hold of a ship. Find the force in the cable if the lorry has:

(a) an acceleration of 0.5 m s^{-2} downwards

(b) a constant velocity of 3 m s^{-1}

(c) a retardation of 0.8 m s^{-2}.

13 The tension in a cable raising a load with an acceleration of 2.5 m s^{-2} is 6 kN. What is the load?

14 A bottle of mass 0.5 kg is released from a submarine and rises to the surface with an acceleration of 0.8 m s^{-2}. If the water offers a resistance of 0.4 N, what is the force of buoyancy forcing it upwards?

15 A balloon which weighs 1 tonne is drifting horizontally.

   (a) What is the total upwards vertical force on the balloon?

   (b) If 100 kg of ballast is thrown out, with what acceleration does the balloon begin to ascend?

16 A balloon which weighs 600 kg is drifting horizontally. Some ballast is then thrown out so that the balloon begins to accelerate upwards at 0.2 m s^{-2}. How much ballast was thrown out?

17

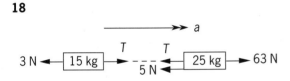

Find a and T.

18

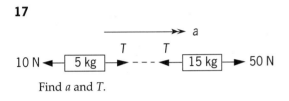

Find a and T.

19

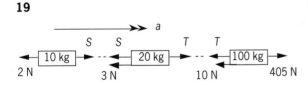

Find a, T and S.

20 Find a and T from the information given in the diagram below.

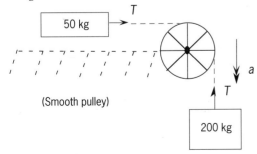

(Smooth pulley)

(Don't forget to put the weight in first!)

21 Find a and T from the information given in the diagram below.

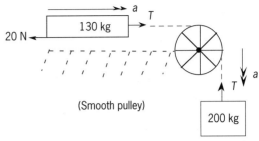

(Smooth pulley)

22

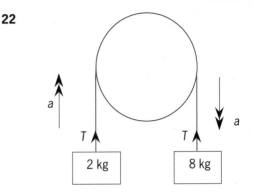

Find a and T

(Don't forget to put the weights in first!)

23 Find T and the missing mass.

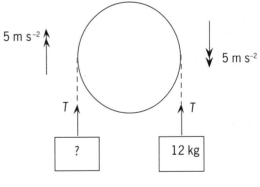

24 A smooth pulley is shown below.

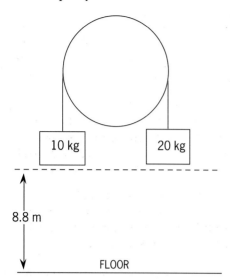

10 kg   20 kg

8.8 m

FLOOR

The weights are released from rest when both are 8.8 m above the floor. The connecting chord snaps after 1.2 seconds so that the 20 kg mass falls freely to the floor.

(a) What is the speed of the 20 kg mass when it hits the floor?

(b) For how long does it fall freely?

(c) What *further time* elapses before the 10 kg mass hits the floor?

25 Two particles of mass 2*m* and 4*m* respectively are connected by a light inextensible string which passes over a smooth fixed pulley. The particles are released from rest with the parts of the string on each side of the pulley hanging vertically.

Find, in terms of *g* and *m* as appropriate:

(a) the magnitude of the acceleration of the particles

(b) the force exerted by the string on the pulley.

26 A light inextensible string passes over a small fixed smooth pulley. The string carries a particle of mass 0.06 kg at one end and a particle of mass 0.08 kg at the other end. The particles move in a vertical plane, with both hanging parts of the string vertical. Find the magnitude of the acceleration of the particles and the tension in the string.

27 (a) A 20 kg mass at the end of a cable is lowered at a rate of 2 m s^{-2}. What is the tension in the cable?

(b) A 30 kg mass at the end of a cable is lowered at a steady speed. What is the tension in the cable?

(c) A 40 kg mass at the end of a cable decelerates at 3 m s^{-2}. What is the tension in the cable?

28 In what time will a force of 8 N reduce the speed of a particle of mass 3 kg from 21 m s^{-1} to 6 m s^{-1}?

29 A dart of mass 0.12 kg flying at a speed of 20 m s^{-1} hits the dartboard and comes to rest in 0.1 seconds. What is the average force exerted by the dartboard on the dart?

30 A cup of 90 grammes is dropped from a height of 1.25 m. What impulse does it receive on striking the floor if it does not rebound?

31 A batsman receives a cricket ball of mass 160 grammes at a speed of 6 m s^{-1} and returns it straight back to the bowler at 12 m s^{-1}. What impulse does the bat give to the ball?

32 A coin of mass 5 grammes is shoved across a board. It receives an initial impulse of 0.01 N s and stops after sliding 0.5 m. Find the deceleration.

33 Sand falls steadily through a hole on to a conveyor belt moving horizontally. 4 kg of sand falls every second, striking the belt at 10 m s^{-1}. Assuming that the sand does not bounce on impact, find the vertical force exerted by the belt on the sand.

34

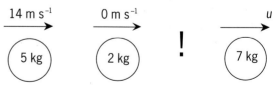

14 m s^{-1} 0 m s^{-1} *u*

5 kg   2 kg   !   7 kg

Find:

(a) *u*

(b) the impulse received by the 2 kg mass.

35

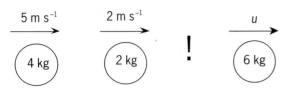

Find:

(a) u

(b) the impulse received by the 2 kg mass.

36

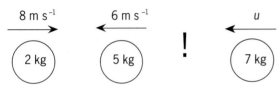

Find:

(a) u

(b) the impulse received by the 5 kg mass

(c) the impulse received by the 2 kg mass.

37

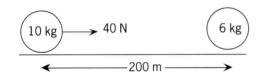

Initially mass of 10 kg and 6 kg are at rest on a smooth horizontal surface. A force of 40 N is now applied to the 10 kg mass for 8 seconds and then removed. Later it coalesces with the 6 kg mass.

Find:

(a) the speed of the 10 kg mass after 8 seconds

(b) the distance covered by the 10 kg mass at that time

(c) the common speed of the combined mass after impact.

38

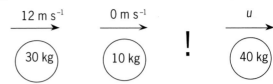

(a) Find the value of u.

(b) If a force of 20 N is then applied in the direction of the motion to the combined mass for 10 seconds, find the distance covered in that time (assuming no resistances).

39 A bullet is fired with a speed of 550 m s⁻¹ into a block of wood of mass 0.49 kg, and becomes embedded in it. If it gives the block a speed of 11 m s⁻¹, find the mass of the bullet.

40 A 20 kg shell is travelling horizontally at 400 m s⁻¹ when it fragments into two masses of masses 8 kg and 12 kg. If the 12 kg fragment has a velocity of 700 m s⁻¹ in the original direction of motion, find the velocity of the lighter fragment.

41 Two pails each of mass 3 kg are suspended at rest by a string passing over a smooth fixed horizontal bar. A brick of mass 1 kg is dropped into one of them from a height of 2.5 m. Find the initial velocity of the pails.

42 A bullet of mass m is fired with a horizontal speed $2u$ into a stationary block of wood of mass $50m$ which is free to move horizontally.

Find the velocity of the block if:

(a) the bullet goes right through it and emerges with speed u

(b) the bullet becomes embedded in the block.

43 A vertical post of mass M is to be driven into the ground. A pile-driver of mass m strikes the post vertically with velocity v. Assuming that the pile-driver does not bounce off the post, prove that the velocity with which the post enters the ground is $\dfrac{mv}{M+m}$.

SUMMARY

In this section we have seen that:

- force is measured in newtons

- steady speed in a straight line means no acceleration (and so no overall force)

- tensions at either end of a taut rope are the same

- weight = mass × acceleration due to gravity or $W = mg$

- force = mass × acceleration or $F = ma$

- problems involving connected particles are best solved by setting up separate equations of motion

- we can model real life situations in this context, e.g. a car pulling a caravan would be modelled by two particles joined by a light inextensible string

- momentum = mass × velocity and it is measured in N s

- momentum after – momentum before = impulse, i.e. $mv - mu = Ft$

- impulse is measured in N s

- during collisions there is a conservation of total momentum

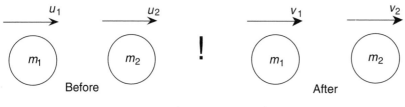

$$\Rightarrow\ m_1u_1 + m_2u_2 = m_1v_1 + m_2v_2$$

ANSWERS

Practice questions A

1   1176 N

2   5 kg

3   (a) 4 m s^{-2} (b) 48 m s^{-1}

4   (a) 3 m s^{-2} (b) 18 m s^{-1}

5   (a) 400 N   (b) 160 m

6   72 N

7   (a) zero   (b) 30 N

8   (a) 260 N   (b) $\frac{1}{3}$ m s^{-2}

9   (a) 78.4 N   (b) 54.4 N

10 (a) 196 N   (b) 236 N   (c) 16 m s^{-1}

Practice questions B

1   $a = 4$ m s^{-2}, $T = 22$ N

2   $a = 4.5$ m s^{-2}, $T = 18.5$ N

3   (a) 980 N   (b) $8\frac{1}{6}$ m s^{-2} (c) $163\frac{1}{3}$ N

4   $a = 7.76$ m s^{-2} $T = 408$ N

5   $a = 3\frac{4}{15}$ m s^{-2}, $T = 130\frac{2}{3}$ N

6   $a = 4.9$ m s^{-2}, $T = 147$ N

7   $m = 12$ kg, $T = 168$ N

8   $m = \dfrac{40(g - a)}{(g + a)}$, $T = 40(g - a)$

9   (a) $a = 4.2$ m s^{-2}, $T = 280$ N

    (b)   560 N

10 4.2 m s^{-2}, 0.28 N

11 14.7 m, $65\frac{1}{3}$ N, 29.4 m

12 (a) 0.9897 seconds   (b) 1.4846 seconds

13 2.45 m s^{-2}, 1 second

14 1 m s^{-2}, $\frac{30}{49}$ seconds

Practice questions C

1 8 N s

2 9 m s^{-1}

3 0.240 Ns (taking g as 9.8 m s^{-2})

4 3 N s

5 5 seconds

6 40 N s

7 1.2 N s

8 20 N s, 1000 N

9 62.5 N

10 (a) 10.6 kg   (b) 159 N s

Practice questions D

1 34 N s

2 20 N s

3 (a) $6\frac{2}{3}$ m s^{-1} (b) $13\frac{1}{3}$ N s

4 $6\frac{4}{7}$ m s^{-1}

5 4 m s^{-1}

6 2 m s^{-1}

7 4

8 7 m s^{-1}

9 2.5 m s^{-1}

10 $v = 4\frac{6}{7}u$

11 0.5 m s^{-1}

12 (a) 8 m s^{-1} (b) 0.12 N s

4

Statics of a particle and motion on an inclined plane

INTRODUCTION   If you put a brick on a plank of wood inclined at 10° to the horizontal, it probably wouldn't slide off. However, if you raised one end of the plank, you would increase the angle of inclination. A point would come at which the brick would begin to slide. In this section we shall be looking at sliding and when it occurs.

When you have finished this section, you should be able to:

- find the resultant of two forces
- resolve a force in two perpendicular directions
- find normal reactions
- understand what is meant by coefficient of friction
- find the maximum frictional force available in any problem
- tackle questions involving equilibrium of particles, including particles on inclined planes
- tackle questions involving both motion and friction with particles moving in straight lines or on inclined planes.

Combining two perpendicular forces   OCR M1 5.7.1 (b)

Let's suppose that two dogs are fighting over a 1.5 kg bone. The first is pulling due North, with a force of 3 N, and the other due East, with a force of 4 N.

Figure 4.1

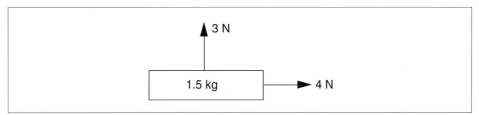

To find out which direction the bone moves, we 'follow the arrows':

Figure 4.2

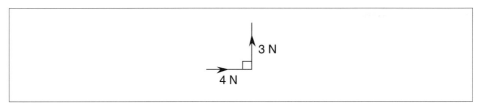

The hypotenuse will then give us the resultant force and lead to the direction of motion.

Figure 4.3

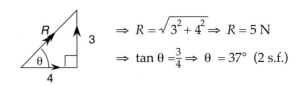

$$\Rightarrow R = \sqrt{3^2 + 4^2} \Rightarrow R = 5 \text{ N}$$

$$\Rightarrow \tan \theta = \frac{3}{4} \Rightarrow \theta = 37° \ (2 \text{ s.f.})$$

And so the bone is really being pulled by a single force of 5N on a bearing of 053°. We can go on to find its acceleration, using $F = ma$:

$$\therefore \quad 5 = 1.5a \Rightarrow a = 3\frac{1}{3} \quad \therefore \text{ Acceleration} = 33\frac{1}{3} \text{ m s}^{-2}$$

You need to be able to find the resultant of two forces and so, before carrying on, spend some time working through a few practice questions.

Practice questions A

1 Find the resultant, in magnitude and direction, of the following sets of forces:

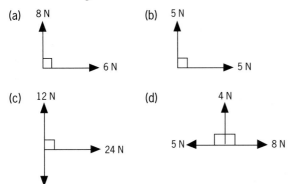

(a) 8 N 6 N

(b) 5 N 5 N

(c) 12 N 24 N 5 N

(d) 4 N 5 N 8 N

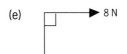

(e) 8 N 15 N

(f) 7 N 24 N

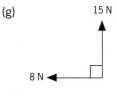

(g) 15 N 8 N

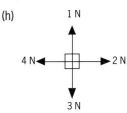

(h) 1 N 4 N 2 N 3 N

2 Find the resultant, in magnitude and direction, of the force **F** where $\mathbf{F} = (15\,\mathbf{i} + 8\,\mathbf{j})$ N.

Resolving a force in two perpendicular directions

OCR M1 5.7.1 (c)

We have just seen, with the example of the two dogs and their bone, that:

Figure 4.4

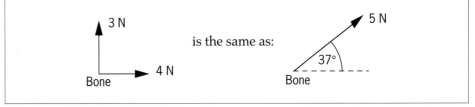

3 N   is the same as: 5 N   4 N   37°   Bone   Bone

It is also important to be able to do the above process in reverse. For that, we need to go:

Figure 4.5

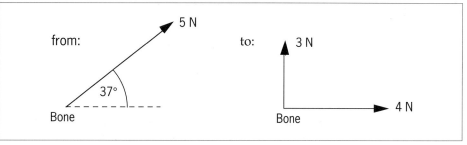

This process is called resolving a force in perpendicular directions. It is a *very important idea* indeed.

Example

A force of 25 N acts at an angle of 30° with the axis Ox as shown.
Find its resolved parts in the direction of the x- and y-axes.

Figure 4.6

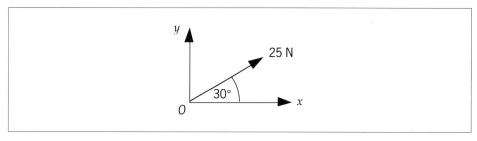

Solution

Begin by drawing a right-angled triangle.

Figure 4.7

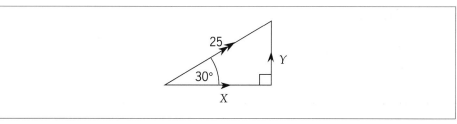

$$\therefore \qquad \cos 30° = \frac{X}{25} \implies X = 25 \cos 30° \implies X = 21.7 \text{ (1 d.p.)}$$

$$\text{and} \qquad \sin 30° = \frac{Y}{25} \implies Y = 25 \sin 30° \implies Y = 12.5$$

Therefore, we can now say that:

Figure 4.8

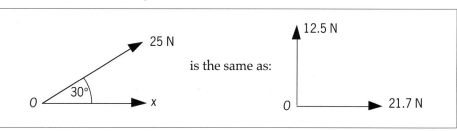

| Example | Find the horizontal and vertical components of the force shown below. |

| Figure 4.9 |

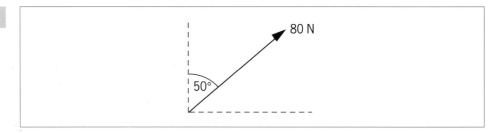

| Solution | Begin by drawing a right-angled triangle. |

| Figure 4.10 |

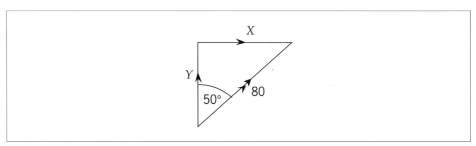

$\therefore \qquad \cos 50° = \dfrac{Y}{80} \Rightarrow Y = 80 \cos 50° \Rightarrow Y = 51.4 \ (1 \text{ d.p.})$

$\therefore \qquad$ The force in the northerly direction = 51.4 N

$\text{and} \quad \sin 50° = \dfrac{X}{80} \Rightarrow X = 80 \sin 50° \Rightarrow X = 61.3 \ (1 \text{ d.p.})$

$\therefore \qquad$ The force in the easterly direction = 61.3 N

Practice questions B

1 Resolve the following forces in the direction of the X and Y axes.

(a)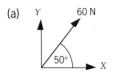

(b)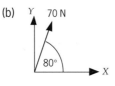

(c) (d)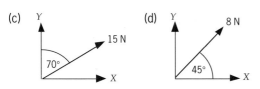

(e)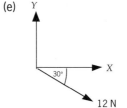

(f)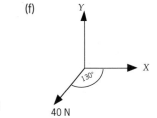

(g)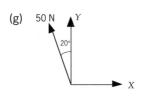

(h)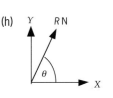

2 Resolve the following forces down the plane (the X direction) and perpendicular to the plane (the Y direction).

(a)

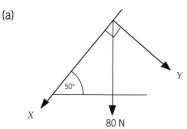

(b)

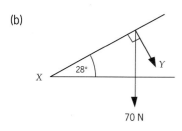

3 A particle of mass 12 kg rests on a plane inclined at 40° to the horizontal.

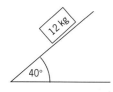

(a) What is the weight of the particle?

(b) What are the components of the weight?
   (i) down the plane
   (ii) perpendicular to the plane?

4 A particle of mass 18 kg rests on a plane inclined at 34° to the horizontal. What are the components of the weight:

(a) down the plane

(b) perpendicular to the plane?

5 A particle of mass m rests on a plane inclined at angle θ to the horizontal

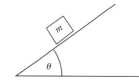

(a) What is the weight of the particle?

(b) Resolve the weight:
   (i) down the plane
   (ii) perpendicular to the plane.

The resultant of any number of forces

OCR M1 5.7.1 (b)

We can now use the previous methods to find the resultant of two forces which aren't perpendicular. Indeed, we can now find the resultant of any number of forces. All we have to do is to find their resolved components and then use Pythagoras.

Example

Find the resultant, in magnitude and direction, of the following forces:

Figure 4.11

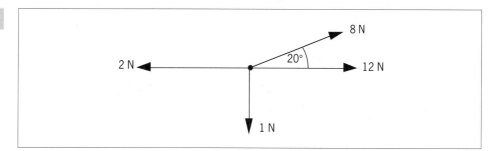

Solution	We begin by finding the resolved components of the 8 N force:

Figure 4.12

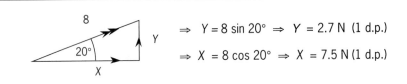

$$\Rightarrow \; Y = 8 \sin 20° \Rightarrow Y = 2.7 \text{ N} \; (1 \text{ d.p.})$$

$$\Rightarrow \; X = 8 \cos 20° \Rightarrow X = 7.5 \text{ N} \; (1 \text{ d.p.})$$

∴ The total force in the easterly direction is:

$$12 + 7.5 - 2 = 17.5 \text{ N}$$

and the total force in the northerly direction is:

$$2.7 - 1 = 1.7 \text{ N}$$

∴ The above four forces reduce to:

Figure 4.13

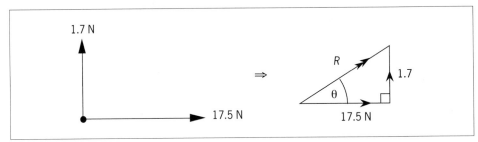

$$\Rightarrow R = \sqrt{17.5^2 + 1.7^2} \Rightarrow R = 17.6 \; (1 \text{ d.p.})$$

$$\text{and } \tan \theta = \frac{1.7}{17.5} \Rightarrow \theta = 6° \; (1 \text{ s.f.})$$

∴ The resultant force is 17.6 N inclined at 6° to the positive x-axis.

Practice questions C

1 Find the resultant, in magnitude and direction, of the following sets of forces:

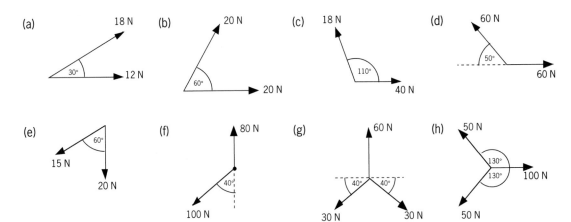

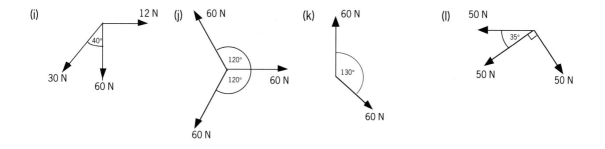

The normal reaction

OCR M1 5.7.2 (d)

Suppose you have a mass of 80 kg and you stand, warming yourself, in front of the fire. Why doesn't your weight of 784 N (80 × 9.8) make you fall through the floor? It's because the floor is holding you up – it is pushing back with a force. But what force? Can it be more than 784 N? Clearly not, otherwise you would be taking off!

Figure 4.14

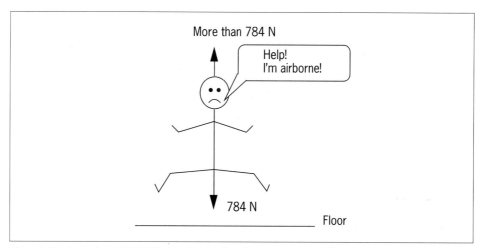

Can it be less than 784 N? Again, it clearly cannot be, otherwise you would be crashing through the floor-boards!

Figure 4.15

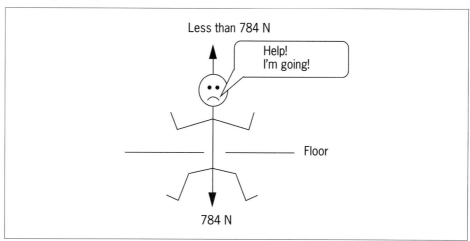

It must then be exactly 784 N.

Figure 4.16

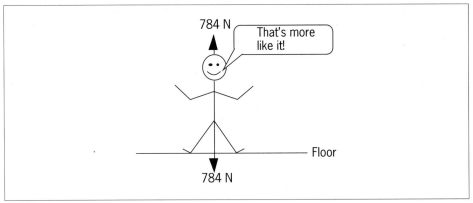

This supporting force from the floor (in this case, 784 N) is called **the normal reaction with the floor.**

This is an example of Newton's Third Law: this states that if a body Y (you) exerts a force on a body F (floor), then F exerts on Y a force **of the same magnitude acting along the same line but in the opposite direction.**

Example

A toy of mass 4 kg rests on the floor. What is the normal reaction?

A child now pushes this toy with a force of 10 N inclined at 40° to the horizontal. What is the normal reaction now?

Solution

The first part is easy.

Figure 4.17

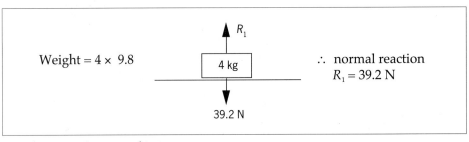

For the second part we have:

Figure 4.18

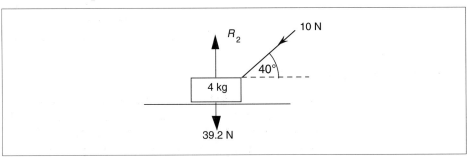

Common sense tells us that the supporting force R_2 must be greater than R_1. Let's find out what it is.

Firstly resolve the 10 N force in two directions:

Figure 4.19

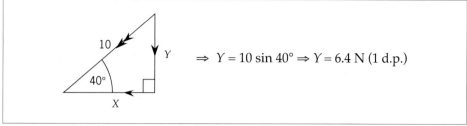

$\Rightarrow Y = 10 \sin 40° \Rightarrow Y = 6.4 \text{ N (1 d.p.)}$

∴ Total downwards force on the toy is:

$39.2 + 6.4 = 45.6 \text{ N}$

∴ Normal reaction $R_2 = 45.6 \text{ N}$

Practice questions D

1 For each of the following, find the normal reaction R. (Remember to add in the weight first of all.)

(a)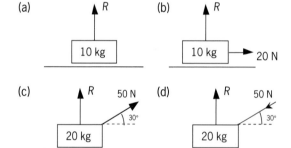

(b)

(g)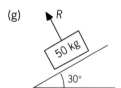

(h)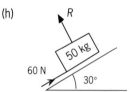

(c)

(d)

(i)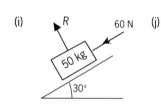

(j)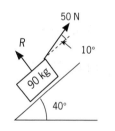

(e)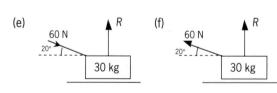

(f)

(k)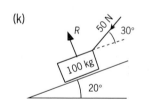

(l)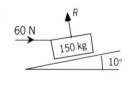

The coefficient of friction

OCR M1 5.7.1 (d)

When two surfaces touch, there may or may not be sliding – it all depends upon the roughness of the surfaces. If you incline a brick at 60° to the horizontal and then place another brick on top, the chances are that it won't slip. However, if you incline a pane of glass at 60° and then place another pane on top of that then, in all probability, it will start sliding. It's all because bricks are rougher than glass.

The amount of roughness between two surfaces is called **the coefficient of friction** and is usually denoted by the Greek letter μ (pronounced 'mew'). The bigger the value of μ, the rougher the surface. Metal surfaces, for example, have a value of μ of about 0.2 and very rarely do surfaces have μ bigger than 1.

The force of friction

OCR M1 5.7.2 (d)

As was said in the introduction, if you put a brick on a plank of wood which is inclined at 10° to the horizontal, it probably won't slide. This is because the frictional force is sufficient to hold it back. However, if you increase the angle of inclination, there will come a time when it will begin to slip. When the brick is on the point of slipping, the **frictional force is just enough to hold it** and the brick is said to be in **limiting equilibrium.** Beyond that, the brick slips away – the frictional force is no longer able to hold the brick.

The biggest frictional force available is μR, when R is the normal reaction. If the frictional force required is less than μR then you won't slip. Beyond that you will either be on the point of slipping or actually moving.

Example

Consider the situation below where a 20 kg mass lies on a flat surface, with coefficient of friction μ. The horizontal force P is applied.

Figure 4.20

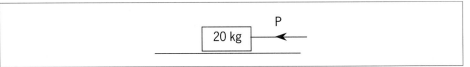

What happens in the following cases:

(a) $\mu = 0.2$, $P = 30$ N (b) $\mu = 0.5$, $P = 98$ N (c) $\mu = 0.6$, $P = 120$ N?

Solution

Let's use a diagram to illustrate what is going on here:

Figure 4.21

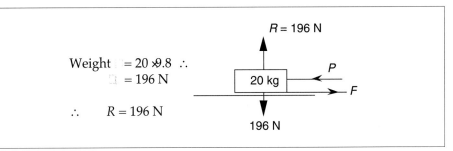

(The frictional force F must act in the opposite direction from which the mass is tending to move.)

(a) $\mu = 0.2$ ∴ Biggest frictional force available

$$= \mu R = 0.2 \times 196 = 39.2 \text{ N}$$

But P is only 30 N ∴ Mass doesn't move.

(b) $\mu = 0.5$ ∴ Biggest frictional force available

$$= \mu R = 0.5 \times 196 = 98 \text{ N}$$

But P is also 98 N ∴ The mass will be on the point of moving.

It will be in limiting equilibrium.

(c) $\mu = 0.6$ ∴ Biggest frictional force available

$$= \mu R = 0.6 \times 196 = 117.6 \text{ N}$$

But P is 120 N ∴ the mass will begin to move under a total sideways force of $120 - 117.6 = 2.4$ N

∴ Using $F = ma$ we get $2.4 = 20a \Rightarrow a = 0.12$

∴ Mass accelerates away at 0.12 m s^{-2}

Example

Consider the situation below where a 40 kg mass lies on a flat surface, with coefficient of friction 0.6. A force P is applied at 30° to the horizontal. What is the least value of P if the mass is on the point of moving?

Figure 4.22

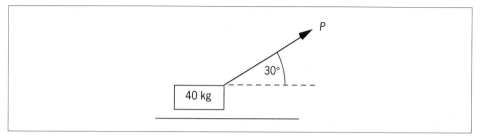

Solution

Resolve P in two directions, and put in the normal reaction R and the maximum frictional force $\mu R = 0.6R$. Not forgetting the weight $40 \times 9.8 = 392$ N, we get:

Figure 4.23

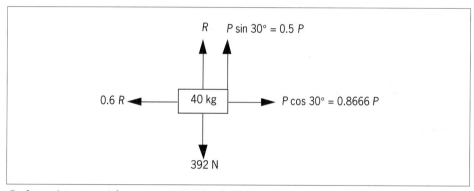

It doesn't move sideways ∴ $0.6R = 0.866P$ ... ①

This is called *resolving horizontally* and is usually written:

    $(\rightarrow)$: $0.6R = 0.866P$ ... ①

It doesn't move vertically ∴ $R + 0.5P = 392$ ... ②

This is called *resolving vertically* and is usually written:

    $(\uparrow)$: $R + 0.5P = 392$ ... ②

Now solve simultaneously to find P.

        equation ② $\Rightarrow R = 392 - 0.5P$

∴   equation ① $\Rightarrow 0.6(392 - 0.5P) = 0.866P$

                           $\Rightarrow 235.2 - 0.3P = 0.866P$

                           $\Rightarrow 235.2 = 1.166P \Rightarrow P = 202$ (3 s.f.)

∴ Force $P = 202$ N.

Example

A mass of 50 kg is placed on a plane inclined at 60° to the horizontal. The coefficient of friction between the mass and the plane is 0.2. When the mass is released, what is its initial acceleration?

Solution	The weight = 50 × 9.8 = 490 N

Its component down the plane is 490 sin 60° = 424 N (3 s.f.) and its component perpendicular to the plane is 490 cos 60° = 245 N.

(Check back to question 5 in Practice Questions B if you are unsure.)

Letting the normal reaction be R (so that the maximum frictional force is $\mu R = 0.2R$) we have:

Figure 4.24

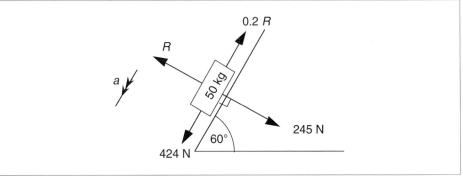

Resolving perpendicular to the plane: $R = 245$

∴ Force down the plane = $424 - 0.2R = 424 - 0.2 \times 245 = 375$ N

Now use $F = ma$ ∴ $375 = 50a \Rightarrow a = 7.5$

∴ Mass accelerates down the plane at 7.5 m s⁻².

Example	A particle of mass 40 kg lies on a rough plane inclined at 60° to the horizontal. A light inextensible string is attached to the particle and passes over a small smooth pulley fixed at the lip of the inclined plane. To the other end of the string is attached a particle of mass 80 kg, which hangs freely. The particles are released from rest with the string taut. If the coefficient of friction between the 40 kg mass and the plane is 0.5, find the initial acceleration of the system and the tension in the string.

Solution	The 40 kg mass has a weight of 392 N with components 392 sin 60° = 339 N (3 s.f.) and 392 cos 60° = 196 N down and perpendicular to the plane respectively. (Refer back to question 5 in Practice Questions B if you are unsure.)

Letting the normal reaction be R (so that the maximum frictional force is $\mu R = 0.5R$) we have the set-up shown in Fig. 4.25.

Resolving perpendicular to the plane: $R = 196$

∴ Maximum frictional force = $0.5R = 98$ N

∴ Total force down the plane = $339 + 98 = 437$ N

∴ The two equations of motion are:

$$784 - T = 80a \qquad \ldots ①$$
$$T - 437 = 40a \qquad \ldots ②$$

Solve simultaneously and get acceleration (a) = 2.89 m s⁻² (3 s.f.) and tension (T) = 553 N (3 s.f.)

Figure 4.25

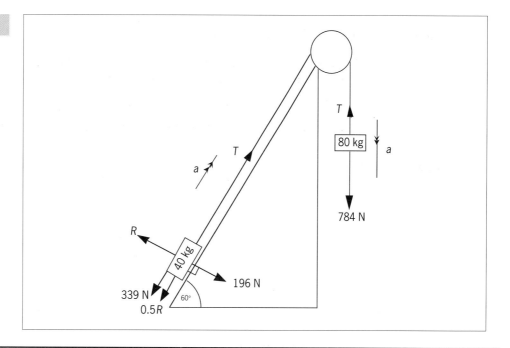

Practice questions E

1 Consider the situation below where a 50 kg mass lies at rest on a flat surface, with coefficient of friction μ. The horizontal force P is applied.

What happens in the following cases:

(a) $\mu = 0.3$, $P = 140$ N

(b) $\mu = 0.3$, $P = 147$ N

(c) $\mu = 0.3$, $P = 160$ N

2 Consider the situation below where a 70 kg mass lies at rest on a flat surface, with coefficient of friction μ. A force P making an angle θ with the horizontal is applied.

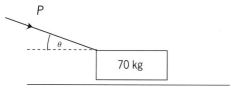

What happens in the following cases:

(a) $\mu = 0.2$, $P = 80$ N, $\theta = 20°$

(b) $\mu = 0.05$, $P = 80$ N, $\theta = 20°$

(c) $\mu = 0.4$, $P = 900$ N, $\theta = 10°$

3 Consider the situation below where a 12 kg mass is being pushed along at a steady speed by a force P inclined at θ to the horizontal.

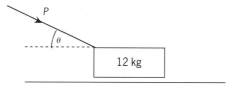

If $\mu = 0.2$ and $\theta = 20°$, what is force P?

4 A 20 kg mass is being pushed along a horizontal rough surface by a horizontal force P.

If $P = 100$ N and $\mu = 0.2$, what is the acceleration of the mass?

5 A particle of mass 8 kg rests on a smooth plane inclined to the horizontal at an angle of 20°. The particle is held in equilibrium by the pull of a string attached to it and inclined to the horizontal at 30°. Find the tension in the string.

If the plane had been rough with a coefficient of friction 0.2, what would the tension be now?

6 The diagrams below show particles in a variety of situations.

(a)

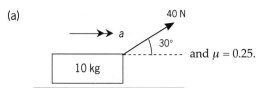

Find the acceleration *a*.

(b)

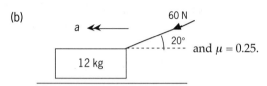

Find the acceleration *a*.

(c)

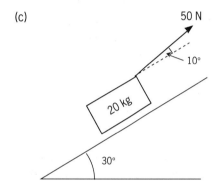

The particle is about to move down the plane. Find μ.

(d)

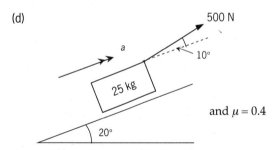

Find the acceleration *a*.

(e)

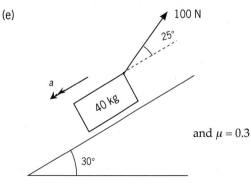

Find the acceleration *a*.

(f)

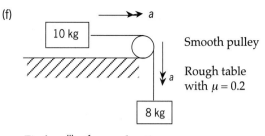

Find: (i) the acceleration *a*

(ii) the tension in the string.

(g)

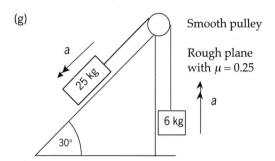

Find: (i) the acceleration *a*

(ii) the tension in the string.

(h)

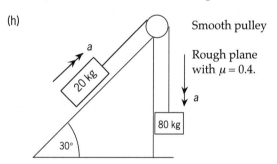

Find: (i) the acceleration *a*

(ii) the tension in the string.

(i)

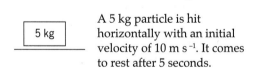

A 5 kg particle is hit horizontally with an initial velocity of 10 m s^{-1}. It comes to rest after 5 seconds.

Find: (i) the retardation

(ii) the coefficient of friction.

(j)

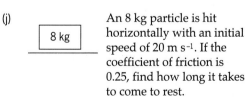

An 8 kg particle is hit horizontally with an initial speed of 20 m s^{-1}. If the coefficient of friction is 0.25, find how long it takes to come to rest.

(k)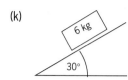

A 6 kg particle is projected up the inclined plane with an initial speed of 20 m s^{-1}. If the coefficient of friction is $\frac{1}{4}$, find how long it will be before the particle comes to instantaneous rest. What happens then?

(l)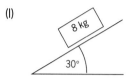

An 8 kg article is released from rest. The plane is rough with coefficient of friction 0.2.

What is the distance travelled down the plane in 2 seconds?

7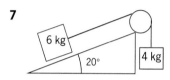

Smooth pulley. The plane is sufficiently rough to keep the system in limiting equilibrium, with the 6 kg mass being on the point of moving up the plane. Find the coefficient of friction.

8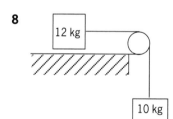

Smooth pulley. The table is sufficiently rough to keep the system in limiting equilibrium. Find the coefficient of friction.

9 A particle of mass 50 kg is at rest on a rough horizontal plane, whose coefficient of friction is 0.7. Find the least pushing force P that will move the particle, where the direction of P is inclined at 30° to the horizontal.

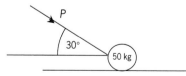

Also find the least pulling force Q that will move the particle, where the direction of Q is inclined at 30° to the horizontal

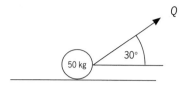

10 A parcel P of mass 3 kg rests on a rough slope inclined at an angle θ to the horizontal, where tan $\theta = \frac{3}{4}$. A string is attached to P and passes over a small smooth pulley fixed at Q. The other end of the string is attached to a weight W of mass 3.2 kg, which hangs freely, as shown below.

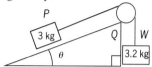

The parcel P is in limiting equilibrium and is about to slide up the slope. By modelling P and W as particles and the string as light and inextensible, find

(a) the normal contact force acting on P

(b) the coefficient of friction between P and the slope.

11 A light inextensible string, passing over a small smooth fixed pulley, carries at one end a weight of mass 3.5 kg, and at the other, two weights each of mass 2.17 kg. If the system is allowed to move, find the acceleration with which the mass of 3.5 kg ascends.

If one of the 2.17 kg masses falls off after the 3.5 kg mass has ascended a distance of 2.1 m, how much further will the 3.5 kg mass ascend?

12 A mass of 4 kg lies at the bottom of a smooth inclined plane 6 m long and 2 m high. It is attached by a light cord 6 m long, which lies along the line of greatest slope of the plane, to a mass of 2 kg, which hangs just over the top of the plane. The system is allowed to move. Assuming that the hanging mass comes to rest when it reaches the ground, find:

(a) the speed of the 4 kg mass just before the 2 kg mass hits the ground

(b) the deceleration of the 4 kg mass after the cord goes slack

(c) the total distance that the 4 kg mass will travel before it first comes to rest.

SUMMARY EXERCISE

Find the resultant, in magnitude and direction, of the following sets of forces:

1

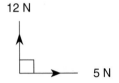

12 N

5 N

2

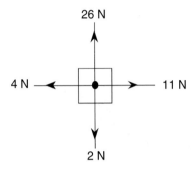

26 N

4 N   11 N

2 N

3

15 N

8 N

4

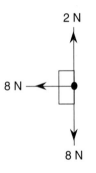

2 N

8 N

8 N

5 Resolve the following forces in the direction of the *x*- and *y*-axes:

(a)

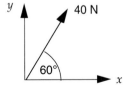

y   40 N

60°   *x*

(b)

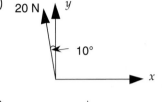

20 N   *y*

10°

x

(c)

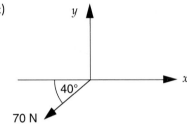

y

x

40°

70 N

(d)

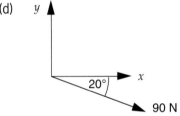

y

x

20°

90 N

6 Find the vertical and horizontal components of the forces shown below:

(a)

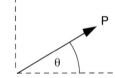

P

θ

(b)

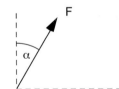

F

α

7 A particle of mass 20 kg rests on a plane inclined at 30° to the horizontal, as shown on the right:

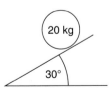

20 kg

30°

What is the weight of the particle? What are the components of the weight

(a) down the plane

(b) perpendicular to the plane?

8 A particle of mass m rests on a plane inclined at θ to the horizontal, as shown on the right:

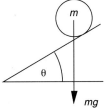

Write down the components of the weight

(a) down the plane

(b) perpendicular to the plane.

In Exercises 9 to 12, find the resultant, in magnitude and direction, of the forces shown. (Give the direction as a bearing taking the y-axis or 'straight up' as due North.)

9

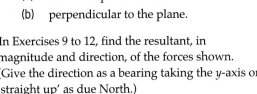

10

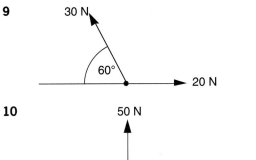

11

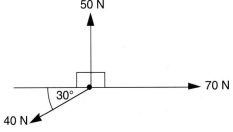

12

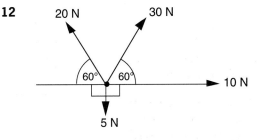

In Exercises 13 to 18, find the normal reaction R:

13

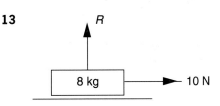

14

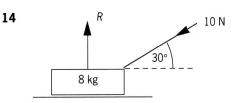

15

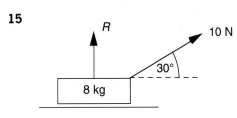

16

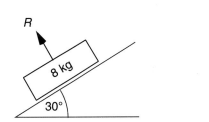

17

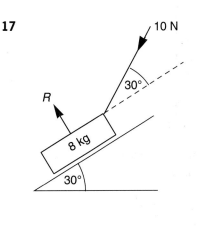

18

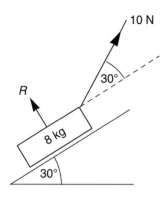

19 Consider the situation below where a 30 kg mass lies at rest on a flat surface, with coefficient of friction μ. The horizontal force P is applied.

What happens in the following cases:

(a) $\mu = 0.5$, $P = 207$ N
(b) $\mu = 0.4$, $P = 110$ N?

20 A floor polisher of mass 5 kg is pushed along the floor at a steady speed; $\mu = 0.7$. If its handle (whose mass is negligible) is inclined at 35° to the horizontal, how hard must it be pushed in the direction of this handle?

21 An ice hockey puck of mass 0.2 kg is hit with a speed of 15 m s⁻¹ and travels 75 m before coming to rest. Find μ.

22 A sofa of mass 50 kg is dragged on to a van up a ramp at 25° to the horizontal. If $\mu = \frac{1}{3}$, what force parallel to the ramp is needed to pull it up at a steady speed?

23 A block of mass 30 kg can just be moved on a rough board by a horizontal force of 98 N. What is the coefficient of friction μ? What force will be needed to move the block if the direction of the force makes an angle with the horizontal of 30°

(a) upwards   (b) downwards?

24 A small body of mass 2 kg rests on a smooth plane inclined to the horizontal at an angle of 25°.

The body is held in equilibrium by the pull of a string attached to it and inclined to the horizontal at 45°. Find the tension in the string and the normal reaction of the plane on the body.

25

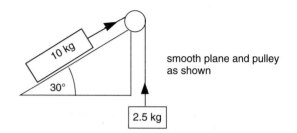

Find the acceleration of the system and the tension in the string.

26 Refer to the diagram in question 25 above. If the plane is now rough, what is the acceleration of the system when $\mu = 0.2$?

27 A particle, of mass M, is placed on a rough horizontal plane. The coefficient of friction between the particle and the plane is μ. A force of magnitude P, acting at an angle θ to the horizontal, is applied to the particle. Show that if this force is just sufficient to pull the particle along the plane, then:

$$P = \frac{Mg\mu}{\cos \theta + \mu \sin \theta}$$

28 A particle A, of mass $4m$, lies on a smooth plane inclined at 30° to the horizontal. A light inextensible string is attached to A and passes over a small smooth pulley P fixed at the top of the inclined plane. To the other end of the string is attached a particle B, of mass m, which hangs freely. The particles are released from rest with the string taut and with the portion AP parallel to a line of greatest slope of the inclined plane.

(a) Write down the equation of motion for particle A down the plane and the equation of motion for particle B.

(b) Hence calculate, in terms of m and g, the magnitude of the tension in the string and the acceleration of the particle A down the plane.

29

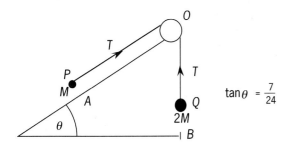

$\tan\theta = \dfrac{7}{24}$

A particle P, of mass M, is held at a point A on a rough plane inclined at an angle θ to the horizontal, where $\tan\theta = \dfrac{7}{24}$. The coefficient of friction between P and the plane is $\dfrac{11}{12}$.

A light inextensible string, of length 50 cm, is attached to P and passes over a small smooth pulley O fixed at the top of the inclined plane. To the other end of the string is attached a particle Q, of mass $2M$, which hangs freely, and is vertically above a point B on the ground, as shown in the diagram above. The distances OA and OB are 32 cm and 43 cm respectively. The particles are released from rest in this position with the string taut and the portion OP parallel to a line of greatest slope of the inclined lane.

(a) Show that while the string is taut the acceleration of P up the plane is $\dfrac{7}{25}g$.

(b) Find the speed, in m s^{-1} to 2 s.f., with which Q hits the ground.

SUMMARY
In this section we have:

- found the resultant of two perpendicular forces by using Pythagoras' theorem
- resolved a force in two perpendicular directions using:

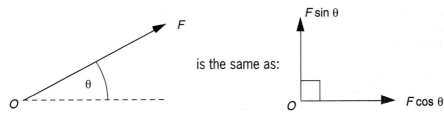

is the same as:

- resolved a weight W on an inclined plane to give:

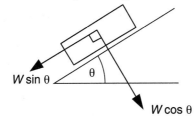

- seen that the normal reaction R is perpendicular to the plane. And so:

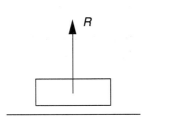

and

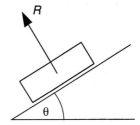

- seen that the maximum frictional force is μR, where μ is the coefficient of friction
- used the fact that the frictional force always opposes the direction of motion
- solved problems involving equilibrium or sliding, both on a horizontal plane and an inclined plane
- used the phrase 'limiting equilibrium' to to mean 'on the point of moving'
- used $F = \mu R$ when a particle is moving or is in limiting equilibrium
- used $F < \mu R$ when a particle is at rest and not about to move off.

ANSWERS

Practice questions A

1 (a)

10 N
53.1°

(b)

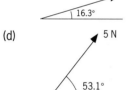
5√2 N
45°

(c)

25 N
16.3°

(d)

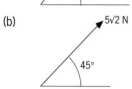
5 N
53.1°

(e)

28.1°
17 N

(f)

73.7°
25 N

(g)

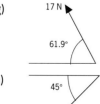
17 N
61.9°

(h)

45°
2√2 N

2

17 N
28.1°

Practice questions B

1 (a) 46.0 N
38.6 N

(b) 68.9 N
12.2 N

(c) 5.13 N
14.10 N

(d) 4√2 N
4√2 N

(e) 10.39 N
6 N

(f)
25.71 N
30.64 N

(g)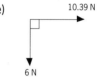
46.98 N
17.10 N

(h)
R sin θ N
R cos θ N

2 (a)
61.28 N   51.42 N

(b)
32.86 N   61.81 N

3 (a) 117.6 N (or 12g)

(b) (i) 75.59 N   (ii) 90.09 N

4 (a) 98.64 N   (b) 146.24 N

5 (a) mg

(b) (i) $mg \sin \theta$ (ii) $mg \cos \theta$
(You need to learn this result by heart.)

Practice questions C

1 (a)
∴

(b)
∴

(c)
∴

(d)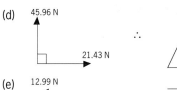
∴

(e)
∴

(f)
∴

(g) 21.43 N (h) 35.72 N

(i)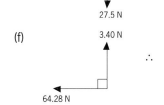

(j) zero resultant

(k)  (l)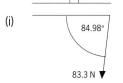

Practice questions D

1 (a) 98 N
  (b) 98 N
  (c) 171 N
  (d) 221 N
  (e) 314.52 N

(f) 273.48 N
(g) 424.35 N (See question 5 in Practice questions B if necessary.)
(h) 424.35 N
(i) 424.35 N
(j) 666.97 N
(k) 945.90 N
(l) 1458.09 N

Practice questions E

1 (a) Remains at rest
  (b) On the point of moving
  (c) Moves off with acceleration 0.26 m s^{-2}

2 (a) Remains at rest
  (b) Moves off with acceleration 0.564 m s^{-2}
  (c) Moves off with acceleration 8.74 m s^{-2}

3 25.0 N

4 3.04 m s^{-2}

5 27.23 N, 12.27 N

6 (a) 1.51 m s^{-2}
  (b) 1.82 m s^{-2}
  (c) 0.30
  (d) 14.05 m s^{-2}
  (e) 0.405 m s^{-2}
  (f) (i) 3.27 m s^{-2} (ii) 52.3 N
  (g) (i) 0.34 m s^{-2} (ii) 60.9 N
  (h) (i) 6.18 m s^{-2} (ii) 289.5 N
  (i) (i) 2 m s^{-2} (ii) 0.20
  (j) 8.16 seconds
  (k) 2.8 seconds. Then slides back down the plane.
  (l) 6.41 m

7 0.346

8 0.833

9 $P = 664.70$ N, $Q = 282.07$ N

10 (a) 23.52 N (b) 0.583

11 1.05 m s^{-2}, 0.959 m

12 (a) $\frac{2}{3}\sqrt{9.8} \sim 2.09$ m s^{-1}
   (b) $3\frac{4}{15}$ m s^{-2}
   (c) $2\frac{2}{3}$ m

5
Moments

A plank is symmetrically placed across a pile of bricks.

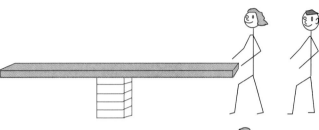

Jo and David decide to sit on the plank, one at each end. Unfortunately David is heavier than Jo, so David crashes to the ground and Jo flies up in the air. This is because David's turning effect is greater than Jo's turning effect.

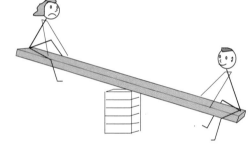

They try again and this time David finds a place on the plank such that he and Jo are equally balanced. They are in equilibrium and David's turning effect is equal to Jo's turning effect.

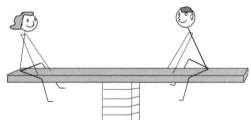

Then David decides to crawl closer to Jo and crash! Jo falls to the ground and David is thrown up in the air. This is because Jo's turning effect is now greater than David's turning effect.

The turning effect of a force therefore depends on the distance of its line of action from the axis about which turning is being considered.

When you have finished this section, you should be able to:

- find the turning effect of a force about an axis

- use the turning effect of a force to solve equilibrium problems.

The moment of a force

Suppose that a light rod is hinged at one end, *A*, and at the other end, *B*, there is applied a constant force of 20 N, always acting perpendicular to the rod *AB*. If the rod has length 4 m then we have:

Figure 5.1

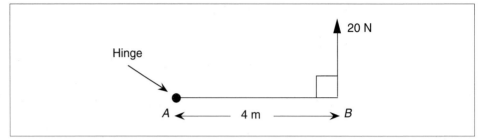

So what happens? Clearly the rod will spin around *A*. The 20 N force has a **turning effect** about *A* and this is called its **moment** about *A*.

In this case the moment is:

$20 \times 4 = 80$ N m anti-clockwise.

In general, the moment of a force *F* about a point *O* is defined as $F \times d$, where *d* is the perpendicular distance of *O* from the line of action of *F*. If *d* is measured in metres and *F* in newtons, then *Fd* is measured in newton-metres or N m.

Figure 5.2

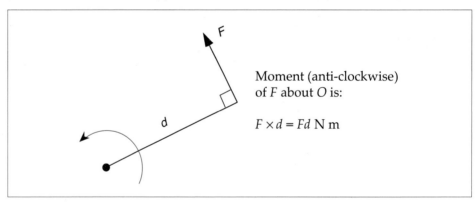

Moment (anti-clockwise) of *F* about *O* is:

$$F \times d = Fd \text{ N m}$$

Example

ABCD is a square of side 4 m. A force of 8 N acts along *BC* as shown.

Figure 5.3

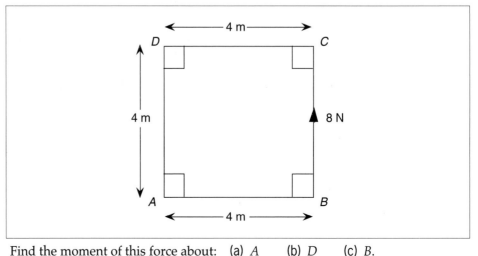

Find the moment of this force about: (a) *A* (b) *D* (c) *B*.

Solution	(a) $A\,\overset{\curvearrowleft}{}$: $8 \times 4 = 32\ \text{N m}$

$(A\,\overset{\curvearrowleft}{})$ is a short-hand way of saying 'the anti-clockwise moment about A'.)

(b) $D\,\overset{\curvearrowleft}{}$: $8 \times 4 = 32\ \text{N m}$

(c) $B\,\overset{\curvearrowleft}{}$: $0\ \text{N m}$

(A force has no turning effect about a point that it passes through.)

Example	A force of 28 N acts as shown. What is its moment about P?

Figure 5.4	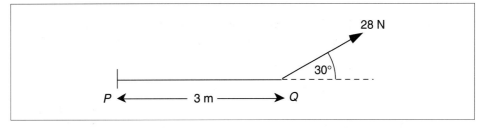

Solution	This resolves as follows (check back to Section 4, Practice questions B) if you've forgotten about resolving):

Figure 5.5	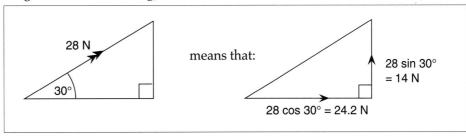

∴ We have:

Figure 5.6	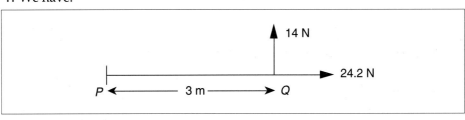

∴ $P\,\overset{\curvearrowleft}{}$: $3 \times 14 = 42\ \text{N m}$

(The 24.2 N force has no moment about P since it passes through P.)

Example

Figure 5.7

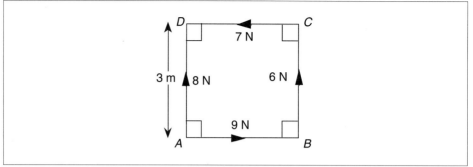

Figure 5.7 shows square *ABCD* of side 3 m. Forces act along the sides as shown. Find their total moment about: (a) *A* (b) *B*

Solution

(a) $A\circlearrowright$: $6 \times 3 + 7 \times 3 = 39$ N m

(The forces 8 N, 9 N have no moment since they pass through *A*.)

(b) $B\circlearrowright$: $7 \times 3 - 8 \times 3 = -3$ N m

(Since the 8 N has a clockwise turning effect about *B*, we need a negative sign.)

Practice questions A

1 Find the anti-clockwise moment of the following forces about the point *P*.

(a)

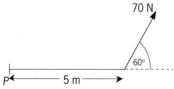

(b)

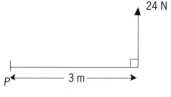

(c)

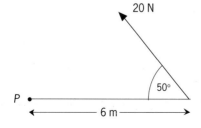

(d) 26 N

(e)

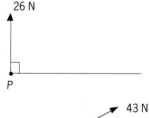

(f) *P* has coordinates (3, 2) and the force is 36**i** N acting at (1, 0). The units along the axes are measured in metres.

(g) *P* has coordinates (6, 2) and the force is (−7**i** + 12**j**) N acting at the point (9, 2)). The units along the axes are measured in metres.

2 Consider the situation below:

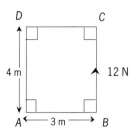

Find the moment of the 12 N force about

(a) A (b) D (c) C.

3 Consider the situation below:

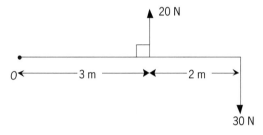

What is the total clockwise moment about O?

4 Consider the situation below:

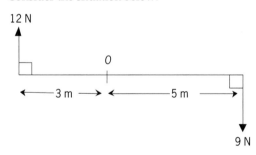

What is the total clockwise moment about O?

5 Consider the situation below:

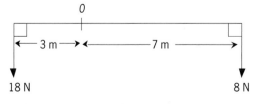

What is the total clockwise moment about O?

6 Consider the situation below:

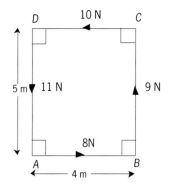

What is the total anti-clockwise moment of the forces about:

(a) A (b) B (c) D.

7 Consider the situation below:

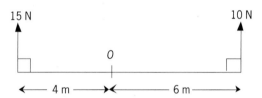

What is the total moment about O?

8 Forces act on a light rod AB as shown below:

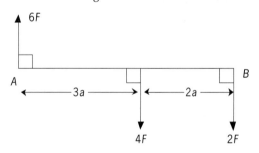

Find their total clockwise moment about:

(a) A (b) B.

9 Forces act on a light rod AB as shown below:

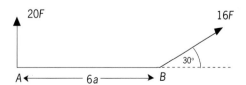

Find their total anti-clockwise moment about A.

10 Forces act on a light rod *AB* as shown opposite.

Find their total anti-clockwise moment about:

(a) *A*   (b) *B*.

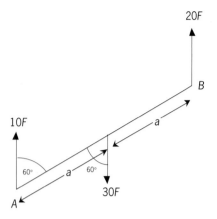

Tackling equilibrium problems

OCR **M2** 5.8.2 (b)

A body is in equilibrium under a system of forces if it doesn't move. It must not move upwards, sideways or turn. And so, under a system of forces, given an equilibrium problem you:

- draw a clear diagram, and put in all the forces that are acting

- resolve upwards and get zero

- resolve across and get zero

- find the total moment about *any* point, and get zero.

The solution will then follow.

| **Example** | The diagram shows a uniform rod *PQ* of mass 5 kg. The rod is 8 m long and is supported horizontally by two symmetrically placed strings attached at *A* and *B*. |

| **Figure 5.8** | |

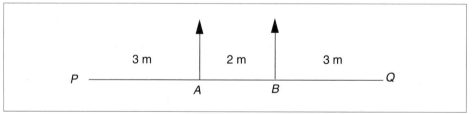

What are the tensions in the strings?

| **Solution** | Rod *PQ* is uniform and so its centre of mass is in the middle of the rod. We therefore take the weight of the rod as acting through this centre. This gives the set-up shown in Fig. 5.9. |

(The tensions *T* will be the same, since the system is symmetrical. The weight of the rod = 5×9.8 N or 49 N.)

$\uparrow : 2T = 49$ N $\therefore T = 24.5$ N

The tension in each string is 24.5 N.

Figure 5.9

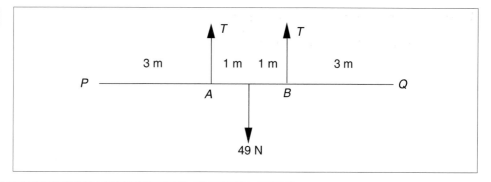

Example

Figure 5.10 shows a non-uniform rod AB of weight 98 N. The rod is 2.2 m long and its centre of mass is 1.2 m from the end A. It is supported horizontally by two strings attached at A and C.

Figure 5.10

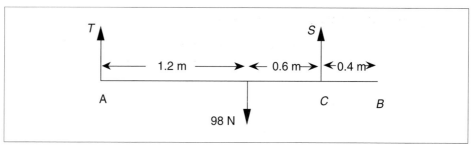

What are the tensions T and S?

Solution

$\uparrow : T + S = 98 \text{ N}$ ...①

$A\,\circlearrowright : S \times 1.8 - 98 \times 1.2 = 0$ ...②

Equation ② gives $S = 65\frac{1}{3}$ N. Then ① gives $T = 32\frac{2}{3}$ N

Example

Figure 5.11 shows a uniform plank AE of length 6 m and weight 90 N. Anne weighs 500 N and sits at A. Brian also weighs 500 N and sits at B. Dusty the dog sits at D and the plank just balances horizontally.

Figure 5.11

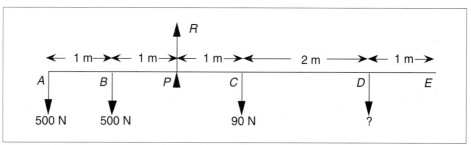

How much does Dusty weigh and what is the normal reaction R?

Solution

Let Dusty weigh W Newtons.

$\uparrow : R = 1090 + W$ ...①

$P\,\circlearrowright : 500 \times 2 + 500 \times 1 = 90 \times 1 + W \times 3$ ...②

(You can take moments about any point you like – I just fancied P!)

Equation ② gives $W = 470$ and ① gives $R = 1560$

∴ Dusty weighs 470 N. (That makes his mass $470 \div 9.8 = 48$ kg. Dusty must be a Great Dane!)

| **Example** | A rod is hinged at A. |

| **Figure 5.12** | |

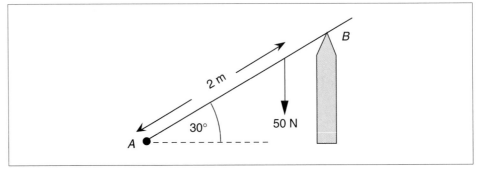

Calculate the distance AB if the smooth support at B exerts a force of 30 N on the rod.

| **Solution** | The normal force of 30 N at B is at right angles to the rod. |

| **Figure 5.13** | |

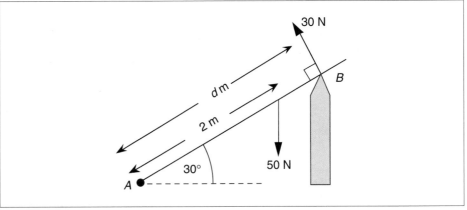

(Look at Section 4, Practice questions D, if you need a reminder about normal reactions.)

The component of the 50 N weight perpendicular to AB is $50 \cos 30° = 43.3$ N. (See Section 4, Practice questions B, for a reminder.)

∴ A↷: $30 \times d = 43.3 \times 2 \Rightarrow d = 2.9$ (1 d.p.)

∴ $AB = 2.9$ m (1 d.p.)

Practice questions B

1 The diagrams below show light rods in equilibrium with distances in metres and forces in newtons. In each case, find the labelled forces

(a)

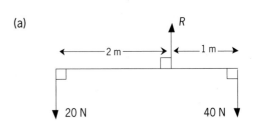

(b)

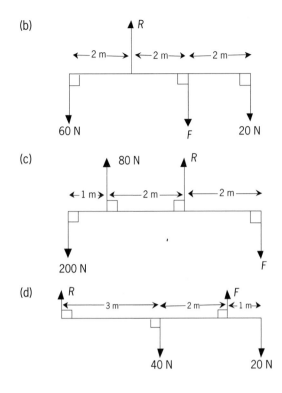

(c)

(d)

(a) Find the magnitude and direction of the force exerted by the plank on the roller at P.

(b) Find the magnitude and direction of the force exerted by the plank on the roller at Q.

(c) State any two assumptions made when you solved this problem.

5 The diagram below shows a uniform rod PQ of length 12 m and mass 8 kg.

A particle of mass 4 kg is attached to the rod at Q. The rod is supported at a point R and is in equilibrium in a horizontal position. Find the length of RQ.

6 A *non-uniform* thin straight rod AB has length $4d$ and mass $5m$. It is in equilibrium resting horizontally on supports at the points X and Y, where $AX = YB = d$ and $XY = 2d$.

A particle of mass $4m$ is attached to the rod at B. Given that the rod is on the point of tilting about Y, find the distance of the centre of mass of the rod from A.

7 Two sisters with masses 50 kg and 45 kg sit at the ends of a see-saw having equal arms of 3 m each. If their brother's mass is 60 kg, where must he sit to balance the see-saw?

8 The diagram shows a uniform gym bench of length 3 m, which stands on a horizontal ground.

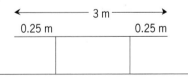

The two supports of the bench are of the same height; they are 2.5 m apart and each is 0.25 m from one end of the bench. When John (who has a weight of 375 N) stands on one end of the bench, it is on the point of toppling. Find the weight of the bench.

2 A uniform shelf of mass 20 kg and length 3 m is hinged at the left end. It is supported at a point 0.5 m from the right end.

(a) What is the supporting force?

(b) If an additional mass of 25 kg is hung from the right end, what does the supporting force become?

3 A girder of negligible mass and length 5 m is suspended in a horizontal position by vertical cables attached at points 0.6 m and 3.6 m from one end. From that end is suspended a mass of 10 tonnes, and from the other a mass of 12 tonnes. Find the tensions in the cables.

4 The diagram below shows a large uniform plank of length 12 m and mass 40 kg held in equilibrium by two small rollers P and Q, ready to be pushed into a cutting machine.

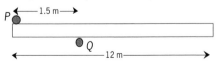

The centres of the rollers are 1.5 m apart and the plank presses up against P and down against Q. The plank remains horizontal are the exerted forces are vertical.

9 Consider the situation illustrated below:

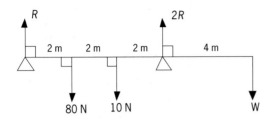

Calculate the values of *R* and *W*.

10 Consider the situation illustrated below:

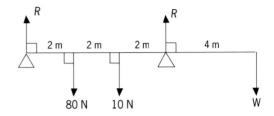

Calculate the values of *R* and *W*.

SUMMARY EXERCISE

1

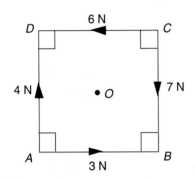

Square *ABCD* of side 4 m.

Forces act along the sides as shown. Find their total anti-clockwise moment about:

(a) *A*

(b) *B*.

(c) If *O* is the centre of the square, what is their total anti-clockwise moment about *O*?

2

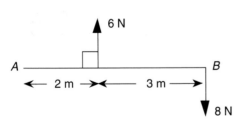

Light rod *AB* of length 5 m with forces as shown. Find their total anti-clockwise moment about:

(a) *A*

(b) *B*.

3

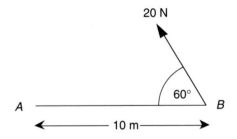

Force of 20 N acts as shown. Find its anti-clockwise moment about *A*.

4

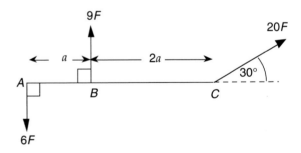

Light rod *AC* of length 3*a*. Forces act as shown. Find their total anti-clockwise moment about:

(a) *A*

(b) *C*.

5 In parts (a), (b), (c) and (d), find the unknown force *F*. In each case the pivot is marked with a cross. (Units are newtons and metres throughout.)

(a)

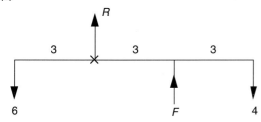

(b)

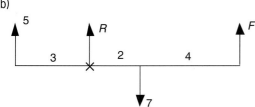

(c)

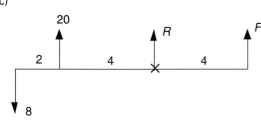

(d)

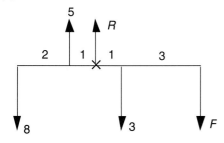

6 A uniform shelf of mass 15 kg and length 4 m is hinged at the left end. It is supported at a point 1m from the right end. What is the supporting force? If an additional mass of 15 kg is hung from the right end, what does the supporting force become?

7 A girder of negligible mass and length 4 m is suspended in a horizontal position by vertical cables attached at points 0.8 m and 2.4 m from one end. From that end is suspended a mass of 6 tonnes, and from the other a mass of 5 tonnes. Find the tensions in the cables.

8 A uniform beam 3 m long has weights 20 N and 30 N attached to its ends. If the weight of the beam is 50 N find the point on the beam where a support should be placed so that the beam will rest horizontally.

9 In parts (a), (b) and (c) the diagrams show an object in equilibrium. Calculate the forces indicated (units are newtons and metres throughout).

(a) Find *X* and *Y*.

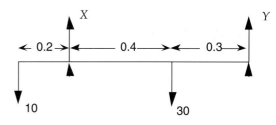

(b) *AB* is a uniform plank weighing 100 N. Find the least force *F* required to prevent the plank overturning.

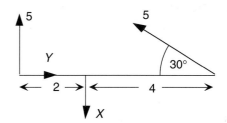

(c) Find *X* and *Y*.

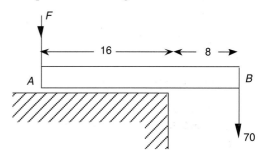

10

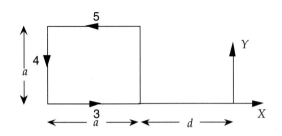

The diagram shows a set of forces in equilibrium.

Find X, Y and d.

11

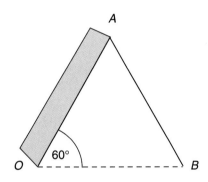

A loft door OA of weight 100 N is propped open at 60° to the horizontal by a light strut AB. The door is hinged at O.

If $OA = OB = 1.2$ m and the weight of the door acts through C where $OC = 0.4$ m, find the force in the strut.

12 The plunger of a pump is pulled vertically upwards, being attached to a point A of a lever ABC, which is pivoted at B. If $AB = 0.2$ m, $BC = 1.2$ m, angle $ABC = 120°$, and BC makes 30° with the horizontal, find the force with which the plunger is pulled up by an effort of 200 N applied at C perpendicular to BC.

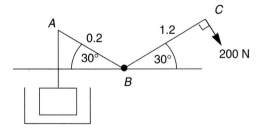

13 A uniform rod AB of weight W is hinged to a fixed point at A. It is held horizontally by a string at B as shown.

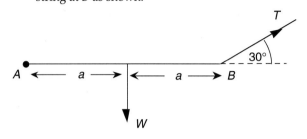

Find, in terms of W, the tension, T, in the string.

14

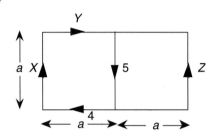

The system of forces shown is in equilibrium. Find X, Y and Z.

15

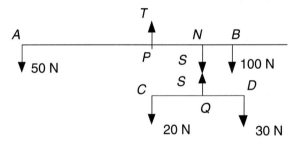

AB and CD are two light rods of lengths 11 m and 5 m respectively. The rod AB is suspended from point P by a vertical string under tension T. The rod CD is suspended from point Q by a vertical string QN under tension S; N is a point on AB. The rods AB and CD hang horizontally. If $AP = 8$ m, find:

(a)   distance CQ (c)   distance PN

(b)   tension S (d)   tension T.

16 A diving board of mass 150 kg is clamped at one end. A diver of mass 75 kg walks gently along the board, which is 3 m long. What turning effect is exerted on the clamp when the diver is:

(a)   1 m from the free end

(b)   at the free end.

SUMMARY

In this section we have:

- seen that the turning effect of a force is called its moment
- found the moment of a force about various axes. For example

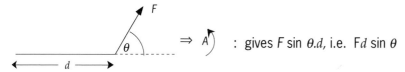

and

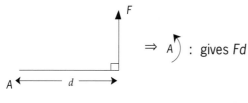

- tackled equilibrium problems by:

  (a) resolving ↑ and getting zero

  (b) resolving → and getting zero

  (c) finding the total moment about *any* point and getting zero.

ANSWERS

Practice questions A

1 (a) 72 N m

(b) 175 √3 N m ~ 303.1 N m

(c) 91.9 N m

(d) 0

(e) 0

(f) 72 N m

(g) 36 N m

2 A ⤴ : 36 N m

D ⤴ : 36 N m

C ⤴ : 0

3 90 N m

4 81 N m

5 2 N m

6 (a) 86 N m

(b) 94 N m

(c) 76 N m

7 0

8 (a) 22*Fa*

(b) 22*Fa*

9 48*Fa*

10 (a) 5√3*Fa* ~ 8.66*Fa*

(b) 5√3*Fa* ~ 8.66*Fa*

Practice questions B

1 (a) $R = 60$ N

(b) $R = 100$ N, $F = 20$ N

(c) $R = 340$ N, $F = 220$ N

(d) $R = 12$ N, $F = 48$ N

2 (a) $12g$ or 117.6 N

(b) $42g$ or 411.6 N

3 $15\ 600g \sim 152\ 880$ N and $6400g \sim 62\ 720$ N

4 (a) $120g \sim 1176$ N upwards

(b) $160g \sim 1568$ N downwards

(c) Plank was a uniform thin rod.
Rollers were particles.

5 4 m

6 $2.2d$

7 2.75 m away from the lighter sister

8 75 N

9 $R = 38\frac{8}{9}$ N and $W = 26\frac{2}{3}$ N

10 $R = 50$ N and $W = 10$ N

Vectors in mechanics

INTRODUCTION   We first came across vectors and vector notation in Section 1. It is the aim of this section to show how vector methods can be used in all the topics so far covered. It should provide some useful revision.

When you have finished this section, you should be able to use vectors in problems involving velocity, acceleration and force.

Velocity as a vector

OCR M1 5.7.2 (a)

Suppose that particle Q is moving and its components of velocity are 5 m s^{-1} in the direction of the positive x-axis and 6 m s^{-1} in the direction of the positive y-axis. The velocity vector of Q can then be written as $(5\mathbf{i} + 6\mathbf{j})$ m s^{-1}.

Acceleration as a vector

OCR M1 5.7.2 (a)

An acceleration vector such as $(7\mathbf{i} - 8\mathbf{j})$ m s^{-2} means that the components of acceleration are 7 m s^{-2} in the direction of the positive x-axis and 8 m s^{-2} in the direction of the negative y-axis.

Example   A particle is moving with a speed of 26 m s^{-1} along the straight line AB. The coordinates of A and B, measured in metres, are given respectively by $(3, 4)$ and $(8, 16)$. Find the velocity vector of the particle.

Solution   Since A and B have coordinates $(3, 4)$ and $(8, 16)$ respectively,

$$\overrightarrow{AB} = \begin{pmatrix} 5 \\ 12 \end{pmatrix} \text{ and } \mid \overrightarrow{AB} \mid = \sqrt{5^2 + 12^2} = 13$$

$\therefore$ A **unit vector** in the direction $\overrightarrow{AB}$ is given by $\frac{1}{13} \begin{pmatrix} 5 \\ 12 \end{pmatrix}$

Since the speed of the particle is 26 m s^{-1}, its velocity vector will be

$$26 \times \frac{1}{13} \begin{pmatrix} 5 \\ 12 \end{pmatrix} = 2 \begin{pmatrix} 5 \\ 12 \end{pmatrix} = \begin{pmatrix} 10 \\ 24 \end{pmatrix}$$

$\therefore$ The velocity vector of the particle is $(10\mathbf{i} + 24\mathbf{j})$ m s^{-1}.

Example	A particle, initially at the origin, has velocity vector $(2\mathbf{i} + 7\mathbf{j})$ m s^{-1}. Find the position vector of the particle 3 seconds later.

Solution	In the x-direction, $s = ut + \frac{1}{2}at^2$ $\Rightarrow s = ut$ (because zero acceleration)

$$\Rightarrow x = 2 \times 3 = 6$$

In the y-direction, $s = ut + \frac{1}{2}at^2$ $\Rightarrow s = ut$ (because zero acceleration)

$$\Rightarrow y = 7 \times 3 = 21$$

$\therefore$ The position vector of the particle is $(6\mathbf{i} + 21\mathbf{j})$ m.

[A *more direct approach* would be to say that, since there is no acceleration, the position vector is given by $\mathbf{u}t$ where $\mathbf{u} = (2\mathbf{i} + 7\mathbf{j})$ m s^{-1} and $t = 3$ seconds.

$\therefore$ The position vector $= (2\mathbf{i} + 7\mathbf{j}) \times 3 = (6\mathbf{i} + 21\mathbf{j})$ m.]

Example	A particle, initially at the point whose position vector is $(\mathbf{i} + 2\mathbf{j})$ m, has velocity vector $(4\mathbf{i} - 3\mathbf{j})$ m s^{-1}. Find the position vector of the particle 4 seconds later.

Solution	The position vector of the particle 4 seconds later is given by:

$$(\mathbf{i} + 2\mathbf{j}) + (4\mathbf{i} - 3\mathbf{j}) \times 4 = \mathbf{i} + 2\mathbf{j} + 16\mathbf{i} - 12\mathbf{j} = 17\mathbf{i} - 10\mathbf{j}$$

$\therefore$ The position vector $= (17\mathbf{i} - 10\mathbf{j})$ m.

Practice questions A

1 A particle is moving parallel to the positive x-axis with speed 7 m s^{-1}. Write down the velocity vector of the particle.

2 A particle is moving parallel to the positive y-axis with speed 8 m s^{-1}. Write down the velocity vector of the particle.

3 A particle is moving with a speed of 15 m s^{-1} along the straight line AB. The coordinates of A are (1, 2) and the coordinates of B are (4, 6), with the particle moving from A to B. Find the velocity vector of the particle.

4 The velocity of a particle has the components 6 m s^{-1} parallel to the negative x-axis and 5 m s^{-1} parallel to the positive y-axis. Write down the velocity vector of the particle.

5 A particle is accelerating parallel to the positive x-axis at 12 m s^{-2}. Write down the acceleration vector of the particle.

6 A particle is accelerating at 26 m s^{-2} along the straight line PQ. The coordinates of P are (0, 1) and the coordinates of Q are (5, 13), with the particle moving from P to Q. Find the acceleration vector of the particle.

7 A particle moving in a straight line has initial velocity vector $(2\mathbf{i} + 6\mathbf{j})$ m s^{-1} and, 5 seconds later, a velocity vector of $(9\mathbf{i} - 2\mathbf{j})$ m s^{-1}. Assuming constant acceleration, find the acceleration vector of the particle.

8 A particle, initially at the origin, has velocity vector $(5\mathbf{i} - \mathbf{j})$ m s^{-1}. Find the position vector of the particle 8 seconds later.

9 A particle, initially at the point whose position vector is $(4\mathbf{i} + 7\mathbf{j})$ m, has velocity vector $(2\mathbf{i} - 3\mathbf{j})$ m s^{-1}. Find the position vector of the particle 5 seconds later.

10 A particle, moving with constant speed, has position vector $(3\mathbf{i} + 5\mathbf{j})$ m and, 4 seconds later, position vector $(9\mathbf{i} - 3\mathbf{j})$ m. Find the velocity vector of the particle.

Force as a vector

If the resolved components of a force are (say) 9 N in the direction of the positive *x*-axis and 10 N in the direction of the positive *y*-axis, then this force can be written in vector form as (9**i** + 10**j**) N.

Example	A force **F** = (5**i** + 6**j**) N acts at a point *P* whose position vector is (3**i** + 3**j**) m. Find the moment of **F** about the point *A* whose position vector is (**i** + **j**) m.

Solution	It is always a good idea to have a diagram to look at.

Figure 6.1

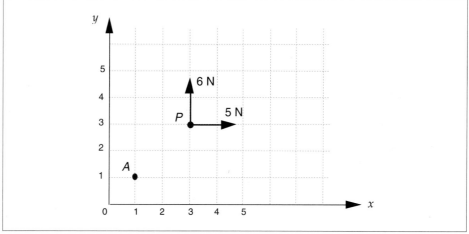

Once you have drawn a diagram, it's back to familiar methods (in this case from Section 5).

$$\therefore \ A \ \circlearrowleft : \ 6 \times 2 - 5 \times 2 = 2 \, \text{N m}$$

⇒ the anti-clockwise moment of **F** about *A* is 2 N m.

Example	A force **F** is given by (5**i** – 12**j**) N. What is the magnitude and direction of this force?

Solution	

Figure 6.2

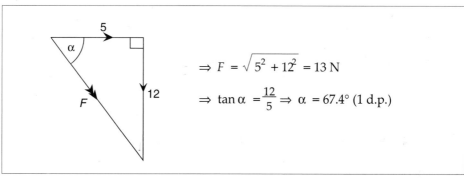

$$\Rightarrow F = \sqrt{5^2 + 12^2} = 13 \, \text{N}$$

$$\Rightarrow \tan \alpha = \frac{12}{5} \Rightarrow \alpha = 67.4° \ (1 \ \text{d.p.})$$

∴   **F** has a magnitude of 13 N and acts on a bearing 157.4˚.

(Unless stated otherwise, it will be assumed throughout that due North is along the positive *y*-axis and due East is along the positive *x*-axis.)

Example	What is the magnitude of the velocity vector $(0.8\mathbf{i} - 0.6\mathbf{j})$ m s^{-1}?

Solution	

Figure 6.3	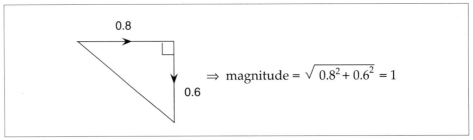

A vector which has magnitude 1 is called a *unit vector*.

Example	A force $\mathbf{F}$ has magnitude 30 N and acts in the direction $3\mathbf{i} + 4\mathbf{j}$. Express $\mathbf{F}$ as a vector in component form.

Solution	

Figure 6.4	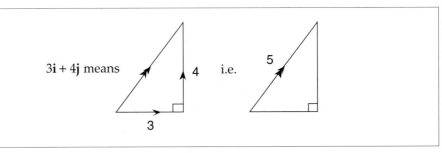

∴ $3\mathbf{i} + 4\mathbf{j}$ has magnitude 5.

But $\mathbf{F}$ is in this direction with magnitude 30 N.

Since $30 = 6 \times 5 \Rightarrow \mathbf{F} = 6(3\mathbf{i} + 4\mathbf{j}) = (18\mathbf{i} + 24\mathbf{j})$ N.

Example	A force $\mathbf{F} = (88\mathbf{i} - 16\mathbf{j})$ N acts on a particle of mass of 8 kg. Find the acceleration of the particle: (a) as a vector (b) in magnitude and direction.

Solution	$\mathbf{F} = m\mathbf{a} \Rightarrow 88\mathbf{i} - 16\mathbf{j} = 8\mathbf{a} \Rightarrow 11\mathbf{i} - 2\mathbf{j} = \mathbf{a}$

∴   (a)   The acceleration vector is $(11\mathbf{i} - 2\mathbf{j})$ m s^{-2}.

(b)   Look at Fig. 6.5.

Figure 6.5	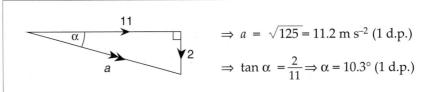

∴   **a** has magnitude 11.2 m s^{-2} and acts on a bearing 100.3°.

| **Example** | A mass of 6 kg has velocity vector **v** = (4**i** + 3**j**) m s^{-1}. Find the momentum of the mass in vector form. What is its speed? |

| **Solution** | Momentum = m**v** = 6(4**i** + 3**j**) N s = (24**i** + 18**j**) N s. |

| **Figure 6.6** | 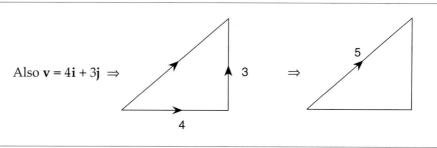 |

$\therefore$ Speed = magnitude of velocity vector = 5 m s^{-1}

| **Example** | A 3 kg mass with velocity vector (10**i** – 3**j**) m s^{-1} hits a 5 kg mass with velocity vector (2**i** + 21**j**) m s^{-1}. After impact they coalesce. Find: |

(a) their common velocity after impact

(b) the impulse experienced by the 3 kg mass during impact.

| **Solution** | (a) Conservation of momentum |

$\Rightarrow$ 3(10**i** – 3**j**) + 5(2**i** + 21**j**) = 8**v**

$\Rightarrow$ 40**i** + 96**j** = 8**v** $\Rightarrow$ **v** = (5**i** + 12**j**) m s^{-1}

(b) Momentum after – momentum before = impulse

$\therefore$ 3(5**i** + 12**j**) – 3(10**i** – 3**j**) = **I**

$\Rightarrow$ 15**i** + 36**j** – 30**i** + 9**j** = **I**

$\Rightarrow$ **I** = (–15**i** + 45**j**) N s, the impulse on the 3 kg mass

| **Example** | A force of (12**i** – 8**j**) N acts on a 4 kg mass, which is initially at rest, at a point whose position vector is (**i** + 3**j**) m. Find the position vector of the mass after 10 seconds. |

| **Solution** | **F** = m**a** $\Rightarrow$ 12**i** – 8**j** = 4**a** $\Rightarrow$ **a** = 3**i** – 2**j** |

Now let's consider the motion in the x-direction ($\rightarrow$) and the y-direction ($\uparrow$):

$\rightarrow$:	u	v	a	s	t	$\uparrow$: u	v	a	s	t
	0		3		10	0		–2		10

$\therefore \quad \rightarrow : s = \frac{1}{2} \times 3 \times 10^2 = 150 \qquad$ and $\uparrow : s = \frac{1}{2} \times -2 \times 10^2 = -100$

But mass was initially at (**i** + 3**j**) m.

$\therefore \quad$ After 10 seconds it will be at (1 + 150) **i** + (3 – 100) **j** = 151**i** – 97**j**

| **Example** | At time t seconds, a particle of mass 5 kg is acted on by a force **F**, where |

$$\mathbf{F} = \begin{cases} 12\mathbf{i} \text{ N} & \text{for } 0 < t \le 6 \\ 4\mathbf{i} \text{ N} & \text{for } 6 < t \le 12 \end{cases}$$

If the initial velocity of the particle was $(\mathbf{i} + \mathbf{j})$ m s^{-1}, find the velocity of the particle:

(a) when $t = 6$

(b) when $t = 12$.

Solution

(a) For $0 < t \leq 6$,

$$\mathbf{F} = m\mathbf{a} \quad \Rightarrow \quad 12\mathbf{i} = 5\mathbf{a} \quad \Rightarrow \quad \mathbf{a} = 2.4\mathbf{i}$$

∴ The acceleration of the particle is 2.4$\mathbf{i}$ m s^{-2} for $0 < t \leq 6$.

∴ The velocity of the particle after 6 seconds is given by

$$\mathbf{v} = \mathbf{u} + \mathbf{a}t \quad \Rightarrow \quad \mathbf{v} = (\mathbf{i} + \mathbf{j}) + 2.4\mathbf{i} \times 6$$
$$\Rightarrow \quad \mathbf{v} = \mathbf{i} + \mathbf{j} + 14.4\mathbf{i}$$
$$\Rightarrow \quad \mathbf{v} = 15.4\mathbf{i} + \mathbf{j}$$

∴ When $t = 6$, the velocity of the particle is $(15.4\mathbf{i} + \mathbf{j})$ m s^{-1}.

(b) For $6 < t \leq 12$,

$$\mathbf{F} = m\mathbf{a} \quad \Rightarrow \quad 4\mathbf{i} = 5\mathbf{a} \quad \Rightarrow \quad \mathbf{a} = 0.8\mathbf{i}$$

∴ The acceleration of the particle is 0.8$\mathbf{i}$ m s^{-2} for $6 < t \leq 12$.

When $t = 12$, *the acceleration has been acting for just 6 seconds* and so the velocity of the particle is given by

$$\mathbf{v} = \mathbf{u} + \mathbf{a}t \quad \Rightarrow \quad \mathbf{v} = (15.4\mathbf{i} + \mathbf{j}) + 0.8\mathbf{i} \times 6$$
$$\Rightarrow \quad \mathbf{v} = 15.4\mathbf{i} + \mathbf{j} + 4.8\mathbf{i}$$
$$\Rightarrow \quad \mathbf{v} = 20.2\mathbf{i} + \mathbf{j}$$

∴ When $t = 12$, the velocity of the particle is $(20.2\mathbf{i} + \mathbf{j})$ m s^{-1}.

The previous nine examples should have given you an idea of the variety of ways vector methods can be used in mechanics. Now it's your turn. Work carefully through the following Practice questions.

Practice questions B

1 A force $\mathbf{G} = (2\mathbf{i} + 7\mathbf{j})$ N acts at a point A whose position vector is $(\mathbf{i} + 6\mathbf{j})$ m. Find the moment of $\mathbf{G}$ about the point B whose position vector is $(3\mathbf{i} + 2\mathbf{j})$ m.

2 A velocity $\mathbf{v}$ is given by $(7\mathbf{i} + 24\mathbf{j})$ m s^{-1}. What is the magnitude and direction of this velocity?

3 A particle P has velocity vector $(8\mathbf{i} + 15\mathbf{j})$ m s^{-1}. Find the unit vector in the direction that P moves.

4 A force $\mathbf{F}$ has magnitude 39 N and acts in the direction $-5\mathbf{i} + 12\mathbf{j}$. Express $\mathbf{F}$ as a vector in component form.

5 A force $\mathbf{F}$ of $(15\mathbf{i} + 23\mathbf{j})$ N acts on a particle of mass 5 kg.

(a) Find the acceleration vector of the particle.

(b) What is the magnitude of this acceleration?

6 A particle of mass 5 kg has velocity vector $(6\mathbf{i} + 7\mathbf{j})$ m s^{-1}. Find the momentum of the particle

(a) as a vector

(b) in magnitude and direction.

Give answers correct to 1 d.p.

7 A particle of 5 kg moving with velocity $(5\mathbf{i} + 9\mathbf{j})$ m s^{-1} hits a particle of mass 9 kg moving with velocity $(5\mathbf{i} - \mathbf{j})$ m s^{-1}. After impact they coalesce. Find:

   (a) their common velocity after impact

   (b) the impulse experienced by the 5 kg mass during impact.

8 A force of $(12\mathbf{i} + 6\mathbf{j})$ N acts on a particle of mass 5 kg. Initially the particle is at rest at a point whose position vector is $(\mathbf{i} + 5\mathbf{j})$ m. Find the position vector of the particle after 12 seconds.

9 The forces $(4\mathbf{i} + 8\mathbf{j})$ N and $F\mathbf{j}$ N, where F is a scalar, act respectively at points whose position vectors are $(3\mathbf{i} + 2\mathbf{j})$ m and $(-\mathbf{i} + \mathbf{j})$ m. The total moment of these two forces about the point with position vector $(\mathbf{i} + \mathbf{j})$ m is zero. Find the value of the scalar F.

10 A particle P has mass 4 kg and moves in a horizontal plane under the action of a constant horizontal force. The velocity of P is initially $(3\mathbf{i} - 6\mathbf{j})$ m s^{-1}, and 3 seconds later is $(12\mathbf{i} + 6\mathbf{j})$ m s^{-1}, where $\mathbf{i}$ and $\mathbf{j}$ are perpendicular horizontal unit vectors. Find:

   (a) the magnitude of the horizontal force acting on P

   (b) the angle this force makes with the vector $\mathbf{i}$, giving your answer in degrees to 1 decimal place.

11 The velocities of two particles P and Q are $(6\mathbf{i} - 2\mathbf{j})$ m s^{-1} and $(8\mathbf{i} + 9\mathbf{j})$ m s^{-1} respectively. Find:

   (a) the speed of P, giving your answer in surd form

   (b) the acute angle between the velocity of Q and $\mathbf{j}$, giving your answer to the nearest degree.

12 Two forces $\mathbf{F} = (3\mathbf{i} + 4\mathbf{j})$ N and $\mathbf{G} = (\lambda\mathbf{i} + \mu\mathbf{j})$ N, where λ and μ are scalar, act on a particle. The resultant of the two forces is $\mathbf{R}$, where $\mathbf{R}$ is parallel to the vector $\mathbf{i} - 2\mathbf{j}$.

   (a) Find, to the nearest degree, the acute angle between the line of action of $\mathbf{R}$ and the vector $\mathbf{i}$.

   (b) Show that $2\lambda + \mu + 10 = 0$.

   (c) Given that $\lambda = 1$, find, to 3 significant figures, the magnitude of $\mathbf{R}$.

13 A force $\mathbf{R}$ acts on a particle, where $\mathbf{R} = (5\mathbf{i} + 12\mathbf{j})$ N. Calculate:

   (a) the magnitude of $\mathbf{R}$

   (b) the acute angle between the line of action of $\mathbf{R}$ and $\mathbf{i}$, giving your answer to the nearest degree.

The force $\mathbf{R}$ is the resultant of two forces $\mathbf{P}$ and $\mathbf{Q}$. The line of action of $\mathbf{P}$ is parallel to the vector $(\mathbf{i} + 2\mathbf{j})$ and the line of action of Q is parallel to the vector $(\mathbf{i} + 3\mathbf{j})$.

   (c) Determine the forces $\mathbf{P}$ and $\mathbf{Q}$, expressing each in terms of $\mathbf{i}$ and $\mathbf{j}$.

14 A particle of mass 8 kg is initially at rest. Suddenly a force of $7\mathbf{i}$ N acts on the particle for 4 seconds and then a reduced force of $4\mathbf{i}$ N acts on the particle for a further 6 seconds. Find the velocity of the particle after:

   (a) 4 seconds

   (b) 10 seconds.

15 A time t seconds, a particle of mass 10 kg is acted on by a force $\mathbf{F}$, where:

$$\mathbf{F} = \begin{cases} 6\mathbf{j} \text{ N} & \text{for } 0 < t \leq 4 \\ 2\mathbf{j} \text{ N} & \text{for } 4 < t \leq 8 \\ 3\mathbf{i} \text{ N} & \text{for } 8 < t \leq 12 \end{cases}$$

If the initial velocity of the particle was $-5\mathbf{i}$ m s^{-1}, find the velocity of the particle:

   (a) when $t = 4$

   (b) when $t = 8$

   (c) when $t = 12$.

Addition of vectors

If Jon is walking along at 1 m s⁻¹ and then walks on to a moving walkway which itself is moving at 1.5 m s⁻¹, his speed will increase to 1 + 1.5 = 2.5 m s⁻¹.

Figure 6.7

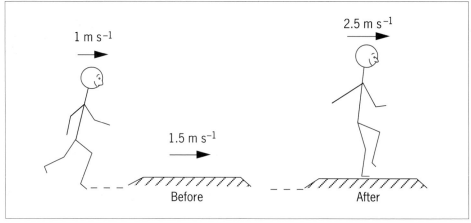

This provides an example where we *add* velocities.

Example

A plane with an airspeed of (7**i** + 6**j**) m s⁻¹ has its speed increased by wind of (−**i** + 2**j**) m s⁻¹. What is the magnitude and direction of the plane's speed now?

Solution

Add the separate velocity vectors to get:

(7**i** + 6**j**) + (−**i** + 2**j**) = (6**i** + 8**j**) m s⁻¹

Figure 6.8

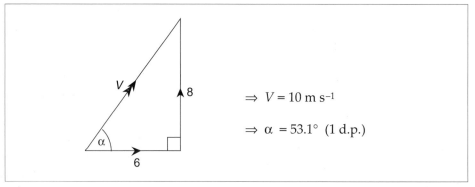

$\Rightarrow V = 10$ m s⁻¹

$\Rightarrow \alpha = 53.1°$ (1 d.p.)

∴ The actual speed of the plane is now 10 m s⁻¹ on a bearing 036.9°.

Practice questions C

1 Forces of (5**i** + 8**j**) N and (6**i** − 4**j**) N act on a particle. What is the total force acting on the particle?

2 A particle with an airspeed of (4**i** + 8**j**) m s⁻¹ has its speed increased by a wind of (−2**i** + 10**j**) m s⁻¹, What is the magnitude and direction of the particle's speed now?

3 Given that 31**i** + 5**j** = λ(2**i** − 5**j**) + μ(10**i** + 8**j**), find the values of the scalars λ and μ.

4 The force **F** is the resultant of two forces **P** and **Q**. The line of action of **P** is parallel to the vector (5**i** + 7**j**) and the line of action of **Q** is parallel to the vector (7**i** + 21**j**).

   If **F** = 16**i** N, determine the forces **P** and **Q**, expressing each in terms of **i** and **j**.

Relative velocities

OCR **M4** 5.10.1 (a)

If Simon is running at 2 m s^{-1} and Annabel is running in the same direction at 3 m s^{-1}, then Annabel's speed relative to Simon's is $3 - 2 = 1$ m s^{-1}.

Figure 6.9

This provides an example where we *subtract* velocities. The rule is:

Velocity of A relative to Y = Velocity of A – Velocity of Y

Example

Particle A is moving with velocity vector $(5\mathbf{i} - 6\mathbf{j})$ m s^{-1}. Particle B is moving with velocity vector $(7\mathbf{i} + 2\mathbf{j})$ m s^{-1}. What is the velocity vector of B relative to A?

Solution

Velocity vector of B relative to A

$\qquad = B$'s velocity vector $- A$'s velocity vector

$\qquad = (7\mathbf{i} + 2\mathbf{j}) - (5\mathbf{i} - 6\mathbf{j})$

$\qquad = (2\mathbf{i} + 8\mathbf{j})$ m s^{-1}

Practice questions D

1 Particle A has velocity vector $(8\mathbf{i} + 12\mathbf{j})$ m s^{-1} and particle B has velocity vector $(10\mathbf{i} + 17\mathbf{j})$ m s^{1}. What is the velocity of B relative to A?

2 Particle A has velocity vector $(2\mathbf{i} + 9\mathbf{j})$ m s^{-1} and particle B has velocity vector $(-5\mathbf{i} + 12\mathbf{j})$ m s^{-1}. What is the velocity vector of B relative to A?

3 Particle A has velocity vector $(5\mathbf{i} + 9\mathbf{j})$ m s^{-1} and the velocity vector of B relative to A is $(\mathbf{i} + 2\mathbf{j})$ m s^{-1}. What is the velocity vector of B?

4 Particle A has velocity vector $(-7\mathbf{i} + 8\mathbf{j})$ m s^{-1} and the velocity vector of B relative to A is $(-\mathbf{i} - 3\mathbf{j})$ m s^{-1}. What is the velocity vector of B?

5 The velocities of two particles A and B are $(9\mathbf{i} - 7\mathbf{j})$ m s^{-1} and $(12\mathbf{i} - 5\mathbf{j})$ m s^{-1} respectively. Find:

(a) the speed of B

(b) the velocity of B relative to A

(c) the angle between this relative velocity and $\mathbf{i}$, giving your answer to the nearest degree.

6 Two rabbits, Alfred and Bertha, are running in a field. The field is a horizontal plane and O is a fixed point on the field from which all position vectors are measured. The perpendicular vectors $\mathbf{i}$ and $\mathbf{j}$ are unit vectors in the plane. At time $t = 0$, Alfred is at the point O and Bertha is at the point with position vector $4\mathbf{j}$ m. Alfred runs with constant velocity towards the point with position vector $(4\mathbf{i} + 3\mathbf{j})$ m, and Bertha runs, also with constant velocity, towards the point with position vector $(8\mathbf{i} + 7\mathbf{j})$ m. Alfred's speed is 10 m s^{-1}, and Bertha's speed is $2\sqrt{73}$ m s^{-1}.

(a) Find Alfred's velocity, giving your answer in vector form

(b) Show that Bertha's velocity is $(16\mathbf{i} + 6\mathbf{j})$ m s^{-1}.

(c) Given that the velocities of the two rabbits remain constant, find, in metres to one decimal place, the distance between the rabbits 5 seconds after they start.

SUMMARY EXERCISE

1 A force is given by the vector $(6\mathbf{i} + 8\mathbf{j})$ N. What is its magnitude and direction?

2 A force $(6\mathbf{i} + 9\mathbf{j})$ N acts on a particle of mass 3 kg. Find its acceleration vector. What is the magnitude of this acceleration?

3 The force $[(a - 8)\mathbf{i} + 6\mathbf{j}]$ N moves a particle parallel to the y-axis. Find the value of a.

4 The force $[8\mathbf{i} + (b + 10)\mathbf{j}]$ N moves a particle parallel to the x-axis. Find the value of b.

5 The force $[(a + 4)\mathbf{i} + (2a - 6)\mathbf{j}]$ N moves a particle parallel to the line $y = x$. Find the value of a.

6 Forces of $(3\mathbf{i} + 2\mathbf{j})$ N, $(4\mathbf{i} + 6\mathbf{j})$ N and $(-2\mathbf{i} + 4\mathbf{j})$ N act on a particle of mass 5 kg. Find its acceleration vector.

7 Forces (in newtons) of $4\mathbf{i} + \mathbf{j}$, $p\mathbf{i} + 3\mathbf{j}$ and $6\mathbf{i} + q\mathbf{j}$ act on a particle of mass 4 kg and produce an acceleration vector (in m s^{-2}) of $8\mathbf{i} + 12\mathbf{j}$. Find the values of p and q.

8 Forces (in newtons) of $4\mathbf{i} + 2\mathbf{j}$, $-2\mathbf{i} + \mathbf{j}$ and $3\mathbf{i} + 5\mathbf{j}$ act on a particle of mass 10 kg.

(a) What is its acceleration vector?

What is the smallest additional force that will move the particle:

(b) parallel to the y-axis

(c) parallel to the x-axis?

9 A mass has acceleration 10 m s^{-2} in the direction $4\mathbf{i} + 3\mathbf{j}$. What is its acceleration vector?

10 A mass has velocity 6.5 m s^{-1} in the direction $-5\mathbf{i} + 12\mathbf{j}$. What is its velocity vector?

11 An impulse has magnitude 20 N s with direction vector $3\mathbf{i} - 4\mathbf{j}$. Express this impulse as a vector.

12 A force has magnitude 12.5 N and acts in the direction $7\mathbf{i} + 24\mathbf{j}$. Express this force as a vector.

13 A 3 kg mass is acted on by forces (in newtons) $3\mathbf{i} + a\mathbf{j}$, $b\mathbf{i} - 5\mathbf{j}$ and $7\mathbf{i} + 7\mathbf{j}$. The mass has acceleration vector (in m s^{-2}) of $3\mathbf{i} + 4\mathbf{j}$.

(a) Find a and b.

(b) After 3 seconds the velocity vector of the mass (in m s^{-1}) is $20(\mathbf{i} + \mathbf{j})$. What was the initial velocity?

14 Initially a particle has a position vector (in m) of $\mathbf{i} + \mathbf{j}$ with a velocity vector (in m s^{-1}) of $4\mathbf{i} + 10\mathbf{j}$.

Its acceleration vector (in m s^{-2}) is constant and is given by $5\mathbf{i} - 2\mathbf{j}$. In its subsequent motion, what is its greatest distance parallel to the positive y-axis and when does this occur?

15 A 4 kg mass has velocity vector (in m s^{-1}) of $3\mathbf{i} + 4\mathbf{j}$. What is its momentum?

16 A 2 kg mass with velocity vector $(1.5\mathbf{i} + 8\mathbf{j})$ m s^{-1} hits a 5 kg mass with velocity vector $(-2\mathbf{i} + 8\mathbf{j})$ m s^{-1}.

They coalesce and move off together. Find:

(a) their common velocity after impact

(b) the impulse received by the smaller mass.

17 A 90 kg missile moves with velocity $(200\mathbf{i} + 100\mathbf{j})$ m s^{-1}.

(a) An explosion sends 50 kg off with velocity $(250\mathbf{i} + 50\mathbf{j})$ m s^{-1} and 40 kg off with velocity $(100\mathbf{i} + 200\mathbf{j})$ m s^{-1}. By considering momentum, explain why this couldn't have been caused by an internal explosion.

(b) In fact, the explosion was caused by another missile of 15 kg hitting the 90 kg missile. If the 15 kg missile was brought to rest by the impact, find the velocity of the missile just before impact.

18 A particle at time t seconds has acceleration vector (in m s^{-2}) given by $\mathbf{a} = 2\mathbf{i} - \mathbf{j}$. Initially the particle is at rest at the point whose position vector (in m) is $3\mathbf{i} + \mathbf{j}$. Find the position vector of the particle at time t.

19 A particle of mass 2 kg moves under the action of a force (in newtons) of $2\mathbf{i} - 6\mathbf{j}$. Initially the particle is at the point whose position vector (in m) is $\mathbf{i} + \mathbf{j}$ with a velocity vector (in m s^{-1}) of $\mathbf{i} - \mathbf{j}$. Find the position vector of the particle at any time t.

20 A particle is acted upon by two forces $(2\mathbf{i} - t\mathbf{j})$ N and $(\mathbf{i} + 4t\mathbf{j})$ N at time t seconds. The particle is initially at rest. Find the momentum of the particle 5 seconds later.

21 The position vector $\mathbf{r}$ cm of a particle at time t seconds is given by $\mathbf{r} = 3(t-1)\mathbf{i} + 4(3-t)\mathbf{j}$
  (a) Using graph paper, draw the path of the particle for $0 \le t \le 4$.
  (b) For what value of t is the particle closest to the origin? [Hint: complete the square.]
  (c) Using (b), calculate the least distance of the particle from the origin.

22 An aircraft with an airspeed of $(5\mathbf{i} - 3\mathbf{j})$ m s^{-1} meets a wind of $7\mathbf{j}$ m s^{-1}. What is the magnitude and direction of the aircraft's ground speed?

23 Particle R moves with velocity vector $3\mathbf{i}$ m s^{-1} and particle S moves with velocity vector $(\mathbf{i} + 6\mathbf{j})$ m s^{-1}. What is the velocity vector of R relative to S?

24 Particle A is moving so that at time t seconds its position vector (in m) is given by $t\mathbf{i} + 3t\mathbf{j}$. Particle B is stationary at the point whose position vector is $2\mathbf{i} + \mathbf{j}$.
  (a) What is the position vector of A relative to B?
  (b) For what value of t is A nearest to B? [Hint: complete the square.]
  (c) What is the shortest distance between A and B?

25 A particle A, of mass 0.2 kg, has a velocity $(16\mathbf{i} - 12\mathbf{j})$ m s^{-1} and collides directly with another particle B, of mass 0.3 kg. Before the collision B is at rest. After the collision B has speed 10 m s^{-1}. Find:
  (a) the unit vector in the direction in which B begins to move
  (b) the velocities, in m s^{-1}, of A and B after the collision
  (c) the impulse, in N s, received by A as a result of the collision.

26 (In this question the velocities given are relative to the earth. The unit vectors $\mathbf{i}$ and $\mathbf{j}$ are directed due east and due north respectively.)

At time $t = 0$, two ice skaters P and Q have position vectors $2\mathbf{j}$ metres and $2\sqrt{3}\,\mathbf{i}$ metres respectively, relative to an origin O at the centre of the rink. The velocity of P is constant and equal to $3\mathbf{j}$ m/s and the velocity of Q is constant and equal to $\mathbf{v}$ m/s. Skater Q moves in a straight line and at time $t = T$ seconds collides with P.
  (a) Give a reason why $-2\sqrt{3}\,\mathbf{i} + 2\mathbf{j}$ is a vector in the direction of the velocity of Q relative to P.
  (b) Show that $\mathbf{v} = -k\sqrt{3}\,\mathbf{i} + (k+3)\mathbf{j}$ when k is a positive constant.

Given that the speed of Q is $3\sqrt{3}$ m/s,
  (c) find the value of k.
  (d) find the value of T.

SUMMARY   In this section we have:

- seen that velocity, acceleration, force, momentum and impulse can be written as vectors
- seen that mass, time and speed are examples of scalars
- used the following formulae:

  $$\mathbf{F} = m\mathbf{a} \qquad \textbf{momentum} = m\mathbf{v} \qquad \textbf{impulse} = m\mathbf{v} - m\mathbf{u}$$

  $$\mathbf{v} = \mathbf{u} + \mathbf{a}t \qquad \mathbf{s} = \mathbf{u}t + \tfrac{1}{2}\mathbf{a}t^2 \qquad \mathbf{s} = \left(\frac{\mathbf{u}+\mathbf{v}}{2}\right)t,$$

  $\mathbf{v}$ (of B relative to A) = $\mathbf{v}$ (of B) − $\mathbf{v}$ (of A)

- seen that the magnitude of a vector can be found by using Pythagoras' theorem
- seen that a unit vector has magnitude 1.

ANSWERS

Practice questions A

1. $7\mathbf{i}$ m s^{-1}

2. $8\mathbf{j}$ m s^{-1}

3. $(9\mathbf{i} + 12\mathbf{j})$ m s^{-1}

4. $(-6\mathbf{i} + 5\mathbf{j})$ m s^{-1}

5. $12\mathbf{i}$ m s^{-2}

6. $(10\mathbf{i} + 24\mathbf{j})$ m s^{-2}

7. $(1.4\mathbf{i} - 1.6\mathbf{j})$ m s^{-2}

8. $(40\mathbf{i} - 8\mathbf{j})$ m

9. $(14\mathbf{i} - 8\mathbf{j})$ m

10. $(1.5\mathbf{i} - 2\mathbf{j})$ m s^{-1}

Practice questions B

1. 22 N m

2. 25 m s^{-1}, making $73.7°$ (1 d.p.) with vector $\mathbf{i}$

3. $\frac{8}{17}\mathbf{i} + \frac{15}{17}\mathbf{j}$

4. $(-15\mathbf{i} + 36\mathbf{j})$ N

5. (a) $(3\mathbf{i} + 4.6\mathbf{j})$ m s^{-2}
   (b) 5.49 m s^{-2} (2 d.p.)

6. (a) $(30\mathbf{i} + 35\mathbf{j})$ N s
   (b) 46.1 N s, making $49.4°$ with the direction $\mathbf{i}$

7. (a) $(5\mathbf{i} + 2\frac{4}{7}\mathbf{j})$ m s^{-1}
   (b) $-32\frac{1}{7}\mathbf{i}$ N s

8. $(173.8\mathbf{i} + 91.4\mathbf{j})$ m

9. $F = 6$

10. (a) 20 N   (b) $53.1°$

11. (a) $\sqrt{40}$ m s$^{-1} = 2\sqrt{10}$ m s^{-1} (b) $42°$

12. (a) $63°$ (c) 8.94 N

13. (a) 13 N   (b) $67°$
    (c) $\mathbf{P} = (3\mathbf{i} + 6\mathbf{j})$ N and $\mathbf{Q} = (2\mathbf{i} + 6\mathbf{j})$ N

14. (a) $3.5\mathbf{i}$ m s^{-1} (b) $6.5\mathbf{i}$ m s^{-1}

15. (a) $(-5\mathbf{i} + 2.4\mathbf{j})$ m s^{-1}
    (b) $(-5\mathbf{i} + 3.2\mathbf{j})$ m s^{-1}
    (c) $(-3.8\mathbf{i} + 3.2\mathbf{j})$ m s^{-1}

Practice questions C

1. $(11\mathbf{i} + 4\mathbf{j})$ N

2. $\sqrt{328}$ m s^{-1} at $84°$ (1 d.p.) with direction $\mathbf{i}$.

3. $\lambda = 3$, $\mu = 2.5$

4. $\mathbf{P} = (30\mathbf{i} + 42\mathbf{j})$ N and $\mathbf{Q} = (-14\mathbf{i} - 42\mathbf{j})$ N

Practice questions D

1. $(2\mathbf{i} + 5\mathbf{j})$ m s^{-1}

2. $(-7\mathbf{i} + 3\mathbf{j})$ m s^{-1}

3. $(6\mathbf{i} + 11\mathbf{j})$ m s^{-1}

4. $(-8\mathbf{i} + 5\mathbf{j})$ m s^{-1}

5. (a) 13 m s^{-1}
   (b) $(3\mathbf{i} + 2\mathbf{j})$ m s^{-1}
   (c) $34°$

6. (a) $(8\mathbf{i} + 6\mathbf{j})$ m s^{-1}
   (c) $4\sqrt{101}$ m ≈ 40.2 m

M1
Practice examination paper

(If a numerical value for g is necessary, take $g = 9.8$ m s^{-2}.)

1 Consider the following:

   (a)   weight

   (b)   mass

   (c)   length

   (d)   tension

   (e)   normal reaction

   (f)   coefficient of friction

   (g)   angle of inclination

   (h)   particle

Which of (a) to (h) are:

   (i)   vectors

   (ii)   scalars

   (iii)   neither vectors nor scalars?

2

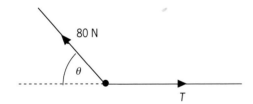

A body of mass 10 kg is held in equilibrium under gravity by two inextensible light ropes. One rope is horizontal, the other is at an angle θ to the horizontal, as shown in the diagram. The tension in the rope inclined at θ to the horizontal is 80 N. Find:

   (a)   the angle θ, giving your answer to the nearest degree

   (b)   the tension T in the horizontal rope, giving your answer to the nearest N.

3 A sprinter runs a 100 metre race. She starts at a speed of 7 m s^{-1}, accelerates uniformly for 2 seconds to her top speed, and then maintains this top speed for the rest of the race. She covers the whole distance of 100 m in a total time of 11 seconds.

   (a)   Sketch the corresponding speed–time graph.

   (b)   Find her top speed.

4 A particle of mass 0.5 kg is moving in a straight line on a smooth horizontal plane under the action of a constant force. The particle passes through the point P with speed 7 m s^{-1} and 10 seconds later it passes through the point Q with speed v m s^{-1}. The distance PQ is 90 m. Find:

   (a)   the acceleration of the particle

   (b)   the value of v

   (c)   the constant force.

5

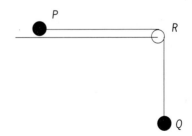

Two particles P and Q, of masses 4 kg and m kg respectively, are connected by a light inextensible string. Particle P is held on a smooth horizontal table. The string passes over a smooth pulley R fixed at the edge of the table, and Q is at rest vertically below R (see diagram above). When P is released the acceleration of each particle has magnitude 5.88 m s^{-2}. Assuming that air resistance may be ignored, find the tension in the string and the value of m.

6 A particle of mass m is moving along a straight line with constant speed $3u$. It collides with a particle B of mass $4m$ moving with constant speed u along the same line and in the same direction as A. Immediately after the collision, the particles continue to move in the same direction, and the speed of B is 5 times the speed of A. Find:

(a) the speed of A immediately after the collision

(b) the impulse exerted by B on A, stating clearly its magnitude and direction.

7 Pirates of old used to punish treachery by making the culprit walk the plank. If the plank used on one such occasion was uniform and of mass 40 kg, of length 6 m, and placed so that 1.5 m projected over the side of the ship, and if the unfortunate man had mass 60 kg, how far did he walk before being tipped into the ocean?

The following day, with the plank still projected 1.5 m over the side of the ship, the man's companion was ordered to walk the plank. But this time, the companion reached the end of the plank without it tipping over. Deduce an inequality that is satisfied by the companion's weight.

8 A boy sitting on a wooden board slides down a line of greatest slope, which is inclined at 8° to the horizontal, on a snow-covered mountain. The combined mass of the boy and the board is 70 kg, and the magnitude of the frictional force between the board and the slope is 130 N. Air resistance may be ignored. Show that the coefficient of friction between the board and the slope is 0.191, correct to 3 significant figures, and verify that the boy and the board are slowing down.

The boy passes a point A travelling at 6 m s^{-1}. Calculate his speed at the point B, where B is 30 m down the slope from A.

Later in the day the boy, still sitting on the board, is pulled up the same slope, with constant speed, by a rope inclined at 35° above the horizontal. The surface of the slope may now be assumed to be smooth. Calculate the magnitude of the force exerted on the board by the slope.

9 A football pitch is a horizontal plane and O is a fixed point on the pitch. The vectors $\mathbf{i}$ and $\mathbf{j}$ are perpendicular unit vectors in this horizontal plane. Peter and Spencer are two players on the pitch. At time $t = 0$, Peter kicks the ball from the origin O with a constant velocity $7\mathbf{i}$ m s^{-1} and runs thereafter with constant velocity $(2\mathbf{i} + 6\mathbf{j})$ m s^{-1}. When Peter kicks the ball, Spencer is at the point with position vector $(10\mathbf{i} + 10\mathbf{j})$ m and starts running with constant velocity $(2\mathbf{i} - 5\mathbf{j})$ m s^{-1}.

(a) Write down the position vectors of Peter and Spencer at time t seconds.

(b) Verify that Spencer intercepts the ball after 2 seconds.

As soon as Spencer intercepts the ball he kicks it, giving it a velocity of $(\lambda\mathbf{i} + \mu\mathbf{j})$ m s^{-1}, when λ and μ are scalars. He aims to pass it to Peter who maintains his constant velocity.

(c) Given that Peter intercepts the ball 3 seconds after Spencer has kicked it, find the values of λ and μ.

M1

Solutions

Section 1

1 (a) $\mathbf{i} + 3\mathbf{j}$ (b) $-2\mathbf{i}$ (c) $3\mathbf{i} - 2\mathbf{j}$
(d) $-2\mathbf{i} + 5\mathbf{j}$ (e) $2\mathbf{i} - 5\mathbf{j}$

2 From *A* to *B* you go 3 along the *x*-axis and 7
up the *y*-axis

$$\therefore \overrightarrow{AB} = \begin{pmatrix} 3 \\ 7 \end{pmatrix} \text{ or } \overrightarrow{AB} = 3\mathbf{i} + 7\mathbf{j}$$

Also $\overrightarrow{BA} = \begin{pmatrix} -3 \\ -7 \end{pmatrix}$ or $\overrightarrow{BA} = -3\mathbf{i} - 7\mathbf{j}$

(Questions 1(e) and 2 have illustrated the following
useful general rule: $\overrightarrow{PQ} = -\overrightarrow{QP}$).

3

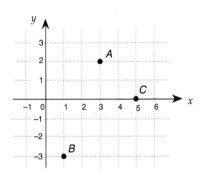

Beginning at *B*, if you go 4 along the *x*-axis and 3 up
the *y*-axis, you finish up at *C*

∴ *C* has coordinates (5,0).

4 *D* has coordinates (3,2). *E* has coordinates (7,10)

$$\therefore \overrightarrow{DE} = \begin{pmatrix} 4 \\ 8 \end{pmatrix}.$$

5 (a) $\overrightarrow{PQ} = \begin{pmatrix} 2 \\ 5 \end{pmatrix}$ (b) $|\overrightarrow{PQ}| = \sqrt{29}$

6 $\overrightarrow{PQ} = \begin{pmatrix} 2 \\ 6 \end{pmatrix} \Rightarrow |\overrightarrow{PQ}| = \sqrt{40}$

7 $\mathbf{a} + \mathbf{b} = \begin{pmatrix} 4 \\ 2 \end{pmatrix} \Rightarrow |\mathbf{a} + \mathbf{b}| = \sqrt{20}$

8 (a) rigid body or particle
(b) lamina
(c) uniform rod or light rod
(d) rigid body or particle
(e) inextensible string
(f) extensible string
(g) particle attached to a rod
  (possibly uniform)
(h) a particle or solid sphere
(i) uniform rod or light rod
(j) a particle flying through the air.

Section 2

1 (a) $\dfrac{30}{2} = 15 \text{ m s}^{-1}$ (b) $\dfrac{-20}{2} = -10 \text{ m s}^{-1}$
(c) 0. At rest

2 (a) Gradient $= -10$ km in 5 min
∴ Velocity $= -120$ km h^{-1} & speed $= 120$ km h^{-1}
(b) 0. At rest

3 (a) $\dfrac{10}{4} = 2.5 \text{ m s}^{-2}$ (b) **Less acceleration**
(c) 12 seconds (d) **2 seconds**
(e) $\dfrac{4 \times 10}{2} + 4 \times \left(\dfrac{10 + 15}{2}\right) + 2 \times 15 + \dfrac{2 \times 15}{2}$
   $= 115$ m

4 (a) $\dfrac{15}{1} = 15 \text{ m s}^{-2}$ (b) $\dfrac{15}{2} = 7.5 \text{ m s}^{-2}$
(The acceleration is -7.5 m s^{-2} but the deceleration
(or retardation) is 7.5 m s^{-2}.)
(c) 1 second (d) $\dfrac{2 \times 15}{2} = 15$ m
(e) $\dfrac{1 \times 15}{2} + 3 \times 15 + \dfrac{2 \times 15}{2} = 67.5$ m

5 (a) $\dfrac{2}{120} = \dfrac{1}{60} \text{ m s}^{-2}$ (b) 5 m s^{-1}
(c) $\dfrac{3}{120} = \dfrac{1}{40} \text{ m s}^{-2}$
(d) $60 \times 5 = 300$ m
(e) $120 \times \left(\dfrac{5 + 2}{2}\right) = 420$ m

6 36 km/h $= 10$ m/s

	u	v	a	s	t
	10	0		60	?

$$\therefore s = \left(\dfrac{u + v}{2}\right)t \Rightarrow 60 = 5t \Rightarrow t = 12 \text{ seconds}$$

7 48 km/h $= 13\dfrac{1}{3}$ m/s and 4 minutes $= 240$ seconds.

	u	v	a	s	t
	$13\dfrac{1}{3}$	0		?	240

$$\therefore s = \left(\dfrac{u + v}{2}\right)t \Rightarrow s = 1600 \text{ m} = 1.6 \text{ km}$$

8

u	v	a	s	t
0	?	9·8	40	

$$\therefore v^2 = u^2 + 2as \Rightarrow v^2 = 0 + 2 \times 9.8 \times 40$$
$$\Rightarrow v = 28 \text{ m s}^{-1}$$

9

u	v	a	s	t
7	13	?		3

$$\therefore v = u + at \Rightarrow 13 = 7 + 3a \Rightarrow a = 2 \text{ m s}^{-2}$$

10 $60 \text{ km h}^{-1} = 16\frac{2}{3} \text{ m s}^{-1}$ and 1 min = 60 seconds.

$\therefore$

u	v	a	s	t
$16\frac{2}{3}$	0.1	?	60	

Find u first. $\therefore$ $v = u + at \Rightarrow 16\frac{2}{3} = u + 6$

$\Rightarrow u = 10\frac{2}{3}$

Now find s $\therefore$ $s = \left(\frac{u+v}{2}\right)t$

$\Rightarrow s = \left(\frac{10\frac{2}{3} + 16\frac{2}{3}}{2}\right)60 \Rightarrow s = 820 \text{ m}$

11

u	v	a	s	t
12.5	0	?	100	

$\therefore$ $v^2 = u^2 + 2as \Rightarrow 0 = 12.5^2 + 200a$

$\Rightarrow a = -0.78 \text{ m s}^{-2}$ (2 d.p.)

$\therefore$ Retardation is $+0.78 \text{ m s}^{-2}$

12 (a)

u	v	a	s	t
30	0	−1.5	?	

$\therefore$ $v^2 = u^2 + 2as \Rightarrow 0 = 30^2 - 3s \Rightarrow s = 300 \text{ m}$

(b)

u	v	a	s	t
30	?	−1.5	273	

$\therefore$ $v^2 = u^2 + 2as \Rightarrow v^2 = 30^2 - 2 \times 1.5 \times 273$

$\Rightarrow v = 9 \text{ m s}^{-1}$

13 (a)

u	v	a	s	t
14	34		?	20

$\therefore$ $s = \left(\frac{u+v}{2}\right)t \Rightarrow s = 480 \text{ m}$

also $v = u + at \Rightarrow a = 1 \text{ m s}^{-2}$. (Needed in (b)!)

(b)

u	v	a	s	t
14		1	240	?

$\therefore$ $s = ut + \frac{1}{2}at^2 \Rightarrow 240 = 14t + 0.5t^2$

$\Rightarrow t = 12 \text{ or } -40$

$\Rightarrow t = 12 \text{ seconds}$

14 After 5 seconds: $s = 2 \times 5 + \frac{1}{2}a5^2$

$\Rightarrow s = 10 + 12.5a$ ... ①

After 6 seconds: $s + 13 = 2 \times 6 + \frac{1}{2}a6^2$

$\Rightarrow s + 13 = 12 + 18a$ ... ②

Solve ① and ② simultaneously and get $a = 2 \text{ m s}^{-2}$

$\therefore$ $v = u + at \Rightarrow v = 2 + 2 \times 6 = 14 \text{ m s}^{-1}$

15 $\downarrow$:

u	v	a	s	t
0		9.8	?	2

$\therefore$ $s = ut + \frac{1}{2}at^2 \Rightarrow s = 19.6 \text{m}$

16 $5 \div 2 = 2\frac{1}{2}$ seconds to reach the top

$\therefore$ $\uparrow$:

u	v	a	s	t
	0	−9.8	?	$2\frac{1}{2}$

Find u first $\therefore$ $v = u + at \Rightarrow u = 24.5 \text{ m s}^{-1}$

Now find s $\therefore$ $s = \left(\frac{u+v}{2}\right)t \Rightarrow s = 30.625 \text{ m}$

17 (a) $\uparrow$:

u	v	a	s	t
0	?	2		10

$\therefore$ $v = u + at \Rightarrow v = 20 \text{ m s}^{-1}$

(b) Ballast has initial velocity of 20 m s^{-1} upwards and is pulled downwards by gravity.

$\therefore$ $\downarrow$:

u	v	a	s	t
−20	?	9.8		10

(The initial velocity downwards is -20 m s^{-1}. A tricky point?)

$\therefore$ $v = u + at \Rightarrow v = 78 \text{ m s}^{-1}$

18 $\uparrow$:

u	v	a	s	t
20	0	−9.8	?	

$\therefore$ $v^2 = u^2 + 2as \Rightarrow s = 20.4 \text{ m}$ (1 d.p.)

19 (a) $\downarrow$:

u	v	a	s	t
0	?	9.8	5	

$\therefore$ $v^2 = u^2 + 2as \Rightarrow v = 9.90 \text{ m s}^{-1}$ (2 d.p.)

$\therefore$ Rebounds with 4.95 m s^{-1}

(b) $\uparrow$:

u	v	a	s	t
4.95	0	−9.8	?	

$\therefore$ $v^2 = u^2 + 2as \Rightarrow s = 1.25 \text{ m}$

20

u	v	a	s	t
0	?	$2g$		10

$\therefore$ $v = u + at \Rightarrow v = 20g \Rightarrow v = 196 \text{ m s}^{-1}$ the additional velocity

21 Suppose they land after the first stone has been falling for t seconds.

$\therefore$ 1st stone:

u	v	a	s	t
0		9.8		t

and 2nd stone:

u	v	a	s	t
11		9.8		$t-1$

They have the same s. Using $s = ut + \frac{1}{2}at^2$ twice we get $0 + 4.9t^2 = 11(t-1) + 4.9(t-1)^2$

$\Rightarrow t = \frac{6\cdot1}{1\cdot2} = 5.08 \text{ seconds (2 d.p.)}$

$\therefore$ Height of cliff $= 4.9t^2 = 4.9 \times 5.08^2$

$= 127 \text{ m (3 s.f.)}$

22 The velocity–time graph is shown below.

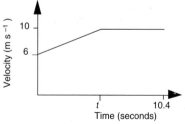

Distance $= 100 \text{ m} \Rightarrow$ area $= 100$

$\Rightarrow t\left(\frac{6+10}{2}\right) + (10.4 - t)10 = 100$

$\Rightarrow t = 2 \text{ seconds}$

$\therefore$ Acceleration $=$ gradient of 1st section

$= \frac{10-6}{2} = 2 \text{ m s}^{-2}$

Distance = area of 1st section

$$= 2 \times \frac{6 \times 10}{2} = 16 \text{ m}$$

23 The velocity–time graph is shown below.

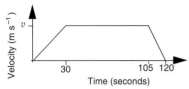

Distance = 2145 m ⇒ area = 2145

$$\Rightarrow 15v + 75v + \frac{15v}{2} = 2145$$

$$\Rightarrow v = 22 \text{ m s}^{-1}$$

Acceleration = gradient $= \frac{22}{30} = 0.73 \text{ms}^{-2}$ (2 d.p.)

24 We get the following velocity–time graph:

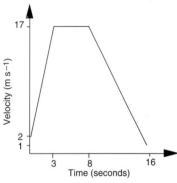

(Gradient of 1st section has to be 5 and we are told that the gradient of the last section is –2.)

(a) Constant velocity = 17 m s^{-1}

(b) Distance covered = area
$$= 3 \times \frac{19}{2} + 5 \times 17 + 8 \times \frac{18}{2} = 185.5 \text{ m}.$$

25 The velocity–time graph is shown below.

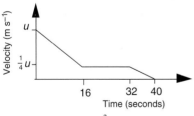

(a) (i) Gradient $= \frac{-\frac{3}{4}u}{16} = -\frac{3}{64}u$

∴ Retardation $= \frac{3}{64}u \text{ m s}^{-2}$

(ii) Gradient $= \frac{-\frac{1}{4}u}{8} = -\frac{1}{32}u$

∴ Retardation $= \frac{1}{32}u \text{ m s}^{-2}$

(b) 1st area $= 16 \times \left(\frac{u + \frac{1}{4}u}{2}\right) = 10u$

2nd area $= \frac{8 \times \frac{1}{4}u}{2} = u$

∴ Total area = 11u, as required

(c) Middle area $= 16 \times \frac{1}{4}u = 4u$

∴ Total distance = 15u = 45 ⇒ u = 3

26

	u	v	a	s	t
A:	u	v	a	s	t
	u		f		t + 10
and B:	u	v	a	s	t
	u		2f		t

Use v = u + at and equate equal velocities.

∴ u + f(t + 10) = u + 2ft

⇒ t = 10 ⇒ A going for 20 seconds

∴ Common velocity at that time = u + 20f

	u	v	a	s	t
∴ A:	u	v	a	s	t
	u	u + 20f	f		20
and B:	u	v	a	s	t
	u	u + 20f	2f		10

Now use $s = \left(\frac{u + v}{2}\right)t$ twice and get

A distance = (u + 10f)20 and

B distance = (u + 10f)10

∴ A distance = 2 × B distance

That was a hard question!

27 (a)

	u	v	a	s	t
P:	u	v	a	s	t
		1	2		t + 4
Q:	u	v	a	s	t
		16	1		t

(Where t is measured from the time that Q starts.)

Using $s = ut + \frac{1}{2}at^2$ twice, Q's distance is greater than P's distance when

$$16t + \frac{1}{2}t^2 > 1(t + 4) + \frac{1}{2} \times 2 \times (t + 4)^2$$

This simplifies to $0 > t^2 - 14t + 40$

$$\Rightarrow 0 > (t - 4)(t - 10)$$

$$\Rightarrow 4 < t < 10$$

∴ Q overtakes P after 4 + 4 = 8 seconds and P overtakes Q after 4 + 10 = 14 seconds

(b) After 8 seconds, common distance = 72 m

(c) After 14 seconds, common distance = 210 m

Another tricky one – especially if you've forgotten how to solve inequalities.

28 (a)

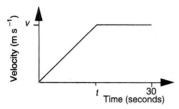

(b) Gradient of first section is 2.3

$$\therefore 2.3 = \frac{v}{t} \therefore v = 2.3\, t$$

(c) Total area = 776.25

$$\therefore 776.25 = \frac{vt}{2} + (30 - t)\, v$$

$$\therefore 776.25 = 30\, v - \frac{vt}{2}$$

Now substitute for v from (b)

$$\therefore 776.25 = 30 \times 2.3\, t - \frac{2.3t \times t}{2}$$

$$\therefore 1552.5 = 138t - 2.3\, t^2$$

$$\therefore 675 = 60t - t^2, \text{ as required.}$$

Section 3

1 (a) $a = 5 \text{ m s}^{-2}$

(b) $\therefore$

u	v	a	s	t	$\Rightarrow v = 20 \text{ m s}^{-1}$
0	?	5		4	

2 (a) $600 = 150a \Rightarrow a = 4 \text{ m s}^{-2}$ $\therefore$

(b)

u	v	a	s	t	$\Rightarrow v = 16 \text{ m s}^{-1}$
4	?	4		3	

3 (a) $F = 60$ N (b) $s = 40$ m

4 $P - 20 = 56 \Rightarrow P = 76$ N

5 (a) $a = 0$ (b) $F = 40$ N

6 (a) $a = 0$ (b) $P = 30$ N.

(c) Then $30 = -8a \Rightarrow a = -3.75 \text{ m s}^{-2}$

$\Rightarrow$ retardation = 3.75 m s^{-2}

7 (a) $F - 200 = 120 \Rightarrow F = 320$ N.

(b) Then $200 = -40a \Rightarrow a = -5 \text{ m s}^{-2}$

$\Rightarrow$ retardation = 5 m s^{-2}

8 $a = 2 \text{ m s}^{-2}$

$\therefore$

u	v	a	s	t	$\Rightarrow v = 12 \text{ m s}^{-1}$
0	?	2		6	

Then $a = -0.4 \text{ m s}^{-2}$

$\therefore$

u	v	a	s	t	$\Rightarrow t = 25$ seconds
12	2	-0.4		?	

$\therefore$ Total time = $6 + 25 = 31$ seconds

9 $a = 2 \text{ m s}^{-2}$

$\therefore$

u	v	a	s	t	$\Rightarrow v = 20 \text{ m s}^{-1}$
0	?	2	??	10	$\Rightarrow s = 100$ m

Then $a = -4 \text{ m s}^{-2}$

$\therefore$

u	v	a	s	t	$\Rightarrow t = 5$ seconds
20	0	-4	?	??	$\Rightarrow s = 50$ m

$\therefore$ Total time = $10 + 5 = 15$ seconds

$\therefore$ Total distance = $100 + 50 = 150$ m

10

u	v	a	s	t	
5	0	?	1.25		$\Rightarrow a = -10 \text{ m s}^{-2}$

Since 400 tonnes = 400000 kg,

$F = 400000 \times 10 = 4$ million N

11

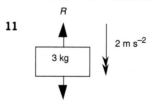

$3 \times 9.8 = 29.4$ N

$\therefore 29.4 - R = 3 \times 2$

$\therefore R = 23.4$ N

12 (a)

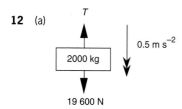

$$\therefore \ 19\,600 - T = 2000 \times 0.5$$
$$\therefore \ T = 18\,600 \text{ N}$$

(b) No acceleration $\therefore \ T = $ Weight $= 19\,600$ N

(c)

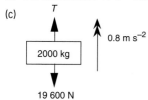

$$\therefore \ T - 19\,600 = 2000 \times 0.8$$
$$\therefore \ T = 21\,200 \text{ N}$$

13

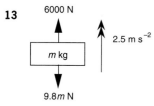

$$\therefore \ 6000 - 9.8m = m \times 2.5$$
$$\therefore \ 6000 = 12.3\,m$$
$$\therefore \ m = 488 \text{ kg (3 s.f.)}$$

(6 kN is shorthand for 6 kilonewtons i.e. 6000 N)

14

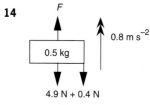

$$\therefore \ F - 5.3 = 0.5 \times 0.8$$
$$\therefore \ F = 5.7 \text{ N}$$

15 (a)

No acceleration $\therefore \ F = 9800$ N

(b)

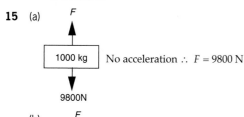

$$\therefore \ 9800 - 8820 = 900a$$
$$\therefore \ a = 1.09 \text{ m s}^{-2} \text{ (2 d.p.)}$$

16 Upwards thrust = weight = 5880 N.
(see question 15)

$$\therefore \ 5880 - 9.8 \text{ m} = 0.2\,m$$
$$\therefore \ m = 588 \quad \therefore \quad 12 \text{ kg thrown out}$$

17 $50 - T = 15a \quad \therefore \quad a = 2 \text{ m s}^{-2}, \ T = 20 \text{ N}$
$T - 10 = 5a$

18 $58 - T = 25a \quad \therefore \quad a = 1.375 \text{ m s}^{-2}, \ T = 23.625 \text{ N}$
$T - 3 = 15a$

19 $395 - T = 100a$
$T - 3 - S = 20a$
$S - 2 = 10a$

Add all three equations to get $a = 3 \text{ m s}^{-2}$
$\therefore \quad T = 95 \text{ N}, \ S = 32 \text{ N}$

20 $1960 - T = 200a \qquad \therefore a = 7.84 \text{ m s}^{-2}, \ T = 392 \text{ N}$
$T = 50a$

21 $1960 - T = 200a \qquad \therefore \ a = 5.88 \text{ m s}^{-2} \text{ (2 d.p.)}$
$T - 20 = 130a \qquad \therefore \ T = 784 \text{ N (3 s.f.)}$

22 $78.4 - T = 8a \qquad \therefore \ a = 5.88 \text{ m s}^{-2},$
$T - 19.6 = 2a \qquad T = 31.36 \text{ N}$

23 $117.6 - T = 60 \qquad T - 9.8m = 5m$

Add these two equations to get
$117.6 - 9.8m = 60 + 5m$
$\Rightarrow 57.6 = 14.8 \ m \ \Rightarrow m = 3.89 \text{ kg (2 d.p.)}$
$\therefore \ T = 57.6 \text{ N}$

24 (a) & (b) $196 - T = 20a \ \therefore \ a = 3.27 \text{ m s}^{-2} \text{ (2 d.p.)}$
$T - 98 = 10a$

$$\therefore \quad \begin{array}{ccccc} u & v & a & s & t \\ 0 & ? & 3.27 & ?? & 1.2 \end{array} \quad \begin{array}{l} \Rightarrow v = 3.92 \text{ m s}^{-1} \\ \Rightarrow s = 2.354 \text{ m} \end{array}$$

Then (free fall): $\downarrow$:
$$\begin{array}{cccc} u & v & a & s \quad t \\ 3.92 & ? & 9.8 & 6.446 \quad ?? \end{array} \quad \begin{array}{l} \Rightarrow v = 11.9 \text{ m s}^{-1} \text{ (2 d.p.)} \\ \Rightarrow t = 0.815 \text{ s (2 d.p.)} \end{array}$$

(c) $: \downarrow :$
$$\begin{array}{ccccc} & u & v & a & s & t \\ & {}^{*}\!-3.92 & & 9.8 & 11.154 & ? \end{array}$$

$\therefore \ v = 15.3 \text{ m s}^{-1} \ \therefore \ t = 1.96 \text{ seconds}$

$\therefore \ $ Extra time $= 1.96 - 0.815 = 1.15$ seconds

(*The clever trick is to regard the 10 kg mass as initially going downwards with a velocity of -3.92 m s^{-1} when the string breaks.)

25 (a)

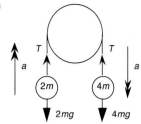

$$4mg - T = 4ma$$

$$T - 2mg = 2ma \qquad \therefore a = \frac{1}{3}g$$

(b) $T = 2\frac{2}{3}mg$

The string exerts the following forces on the pulley:

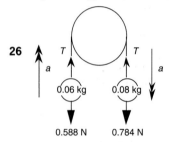

$\therefore$ force exerted by string on pulley $= 2T = 5\frac{1}{3}mg$

(Remember – the tensions at either end of a string are equal and opposite.)

26

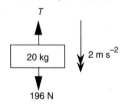

$$0.784 - T = 0.08a$$

$$T - 0.588 = 0.06a$$

$$\therefore a = 1.4 \text{ m s}^{-2}, \ T = 0.672 \text{ N}$$

27 (a)

$$196 - T = 20 \times 2 \quad \Rightarrow T = 156 \text{ N}$$

(b) No acceleration $\Rightarrow T = $ weight $= 294$ N

(c)

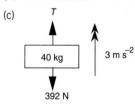

$$T - 392 = 40 \times 3 \quad \Rightarrow T = 512 \text{ N}$$

28 $3 \times 21 - 3 \times 6 = 8t \Rightarrow t = 5.625$ seconds

29 $0.12 \times 20 = F \times 0.1 \Rightarrow F = 24$ N

30 $v^2 = 0^2 + 2 \times 9.8 \times 1.25 \Rightarrow v = 4.95 \text{ m s}^{-1}$ (2d.p.)

$\Rightarrow$ Impulse $= 0.09 \times 4.95 = 0.45$ N s

31 The impulse is away from the bat and so all speeds must have that direction

$\therefore u = -6 \text{ m s}^{-1}, v = 12 \text{ m s}^{-1}, m = 0.16$ kg

$\therefore 0.16 \times 12 - 0.16 \times -6 = $ impulse

$\Rightarrow$ impulse $= 2.88$ N s

32 $0.005u = 0.01 \ \therefore u = 2 \text{ m s}^{-1}$ (initial velocity)

$\Rightarrow 0^2 = 2^2 + 2 \times a \times 0.5$

$\therefore a = -4 \text{ m s}^{-2}$ (acceleration)

33 $4 \times 10 = F \times 1 \Rightarrow F = 40$ N

34 (a) $5 \times 14 = 7u \Rightarrow u = 10 \text{ m s}^{-1}$

(b) $2 \times 10 - 2 \times 0 = $ impulse

$\Rightarrow$ impulse $= 20$ N s

35 (a) $4 \times 5 + 2 \times 2 = 6u \Rightarrow u = 4 \text{ m s}^{-1}$

(b) $2 \times 4 - 2 \times 2 = $ impulse $\Rightarrow$ impulse $= 4$ N s

36 (a) $5 \times 6 - 2 \times 8 = 7u \Rightarrow u = 2 \text{ m s}^{-1}$

(b) $5 \times 2 - 5 \times 6 = $ impulse

$\Rightarrow$ impulse $= -20$ N s

(c) 20 N s

37 $a = 4 \text{ m s}^{-2}$

(a) $v = 0 + 4 \times 8 = 32 \text{ m s}^{-1}$

(b) $s = \left(\frac{0+32}{2}\right)8 = 128$ m

(c) $10 \times 32 + 6 \times 0 = 16u \Rightarrow u = 20 \text{ m s}^{-1}$

38 (a) $30 \times 12 = 40u \Rightarrow u = 9 \text{ m s}^{-1}$

(b) $a = 0.5 \text{ m s}^{-2}$

$s = 9 \times 10 + \frac{1}{2} \times 0.5 \times 10^2 = 115$ m

39 $m \times 550 = (0.49 + m) \times 11 \Rightarrow m = 0.01$ kg

40 $20 \times 400 = 12 \times 700 + 8u \Rightarrow u = -50 \text{ m s}^{-1}$

$\therefore$ velocity of 50 m s^{-1} in the opposite direction.

41 $v^2 = 0^2 + 2 \times 9.8 \times 2.5 \Rightarrow v = 7 \text{ m s}^{-1}$ before impact.

After impact let the 7 kg system be moving with velocity u.

$\therefore 1 \times 7 = 7u \ \therefore u = 1 \text{ m s}^{-1}$

42 (a)

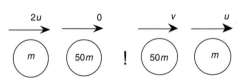

$\therefore m \times 2u + 50m \times 0 = 50m \times v + m \times u$

$\therefore 2\cancel{m}u = 50\cancel{m}v + \cancel{m}u \qquad \therefore v = \dfrac{u}{50}$

(b)

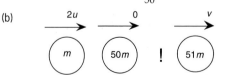

$\therefore m \times 2u + 50m \times 0 = 51mv \ \therefore v = \dfrac{2u}{51}$

43 Let V be the common speed after impact.

$\therefore mv = (m + M)V \Rightarrow V = mv \Big/ (m + M).$

Section 4

1

∴ $R = 13$ N   ∴ $θ = 67.4°$ (1 d.p.)
∴ Bearing $= 022.6°$ (1 d.p.)

2

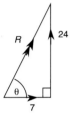

∴ $R = 25$ N   ∴ $θ = 73.7°$ (1 d.p.)
∴ Bearing $= 016.3°$ (1 d.p.)

3

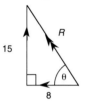

∴ $R = 17$ N   ∴ $θ = 61.9°$ (1 d.p.)
∴ Bearing $= 331.9°$ (1 d.p.)

4

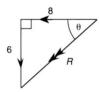

∴ $R = 10$ N   ∴ $θ = 36.7°$ (1 d.p.)
∴ Bearing $= 233.3°$ (1 d.p.)

5 (a)

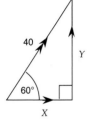

∴ $X = 40 \cos 60° = 20$ N
∴ $Y = 40 \sin 60° = 34.6$ N (1 d.p.)

(b)

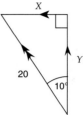

∴ $X = 20 \sin 10° = 3.5$ N (1 d.p.)
∴ $Y = 20 \cos 10° = 19.7$ N (1 d.p.)

(c)

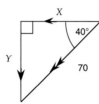

∴ $X = 70 \cos 40° = 53.6$ N (1 d.p.)
∴ $Y = 70 \sin 40° = 45.0$ N (1 d.p.)

(d)

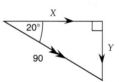

∴ $X = 90 \cos 20° = 84.6$ N (1 d.p.)
∴ $Y = 90 \sin 20° = 30.8$ N (1 d.p.)

6 (a)

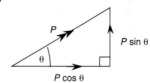

(b)

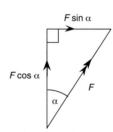

7

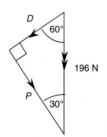

Weight $= 20 × 9.8 = 196$ N.
(a) ∴ $D = 196 \sin 30° = 98$ N
(b) ∴ $P = 196 \cos 30° = 170$ N (3 s.f.)

8

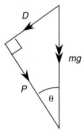

(a) Component of weight down the plane
    = $mg \sin \theta$

(b) Component of weight perpendicular
    to the plane = $mg \cos \theta$

You may have found questions 7 and 8 rather tricky.
I suggest that you learn by heart:

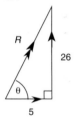

resolves to:

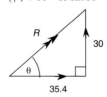

We'll be returning to this result again and again.

9 ($\rightarrow$) : $20 - 30 \cos 60° = 5$ N

($\uparrow$) : $30 \sin 60° = 26$ N

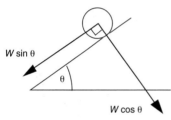

∴ $R = 26.5$ N (1 d.p.) and $\theta = 79°$ (2 s.f.)

∴ Bearing = $011°$ (2 s.f.)

10 ($\rightarrow$) : $70 - 40 \cos 30 = 35.4$ N

($\uparrow$) : $50 - 40 \sin 30 = 30$ N

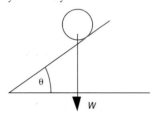

∴ $R = 46.5$ N (1 d.p.) and $\theta = 40°$ (2 s.f.)

∴ Bearing = $050°$ (2 s.f.)

11 ($\rightarrow$) : $40 + 50 \cos 20° - 70 \cos 40° = 33.36$ N

($\uparrow$) : $30 - 70 \sin 40° + 50 \sin 20° = 2.11$ N

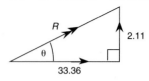

∴ $R = 33.4$ N (1 d.p.) and $\theta = 3.6°$ (1 d.p.)

∴ Bearing = $086.4°$ (1 d.p.)

12 ($\rightarrow$) : $10 + 30 \cos 60° - 20 \cos 60° = 15$ N

($\uparrow$) : $30 \sin 60 + 20 \sin 60° - 5 = 38.3$ N

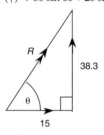

∴ $R = 41$ N (2 s.f.) and $\theta = 69°$ (2 s.f.)

∴ Bearing = $021°$ (2 s.f.)

13 $R = 8 \times 9.8 = 78.4$ N

14 $R = 78.4 + 10 \sin 30° = 83.4$ N

15 $R + 10 \sin 30° = 78.4 \Rightarrow R = 73.4$ N

16 $R = 78.4 \cos 30° \Rightarrow R = 67.9$ N (1 d.p.)

(If this causes trouble, refer back to Exercise 8.)

17 $R = 78.4 \cos 30° + 10 \sin 30°$
        $\Rightarrow R = 72.9$ N (1 d.p.)

18 $R + 10 \sin 30° = 78.4 \cos 30°$
        $\Rightarrow R = 62.9$ N (1 d.p.)

19

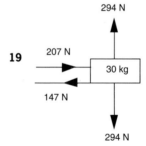

(a) Maximum frictional force
    = $0.5 \times 294 = 147$ N.

    ∴ body moves.

    $F = ma \Rightarrow 60 = 30a \Rightarrow$ acceleration = 2 m s^{-2}

(b) Maximum frictional force
    = $0.4 \times 294 = 117.6$ N

    ∴ Body doesn't move.

20

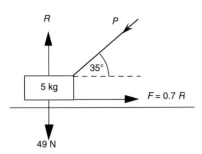

Steady velocity means no acceleration

∴ The forces balance in two directions.

$(\rightarrow) : P \cos 35° = 0.7R$

$(\uparrow) : R = 49 + P \sin 35°$

$\Rightarrow P \cos 35° = 0.7(49 + P \sin 35°)$

$\Rightarrow P = 82 \text{ N (2 s.f.)}$

21

u	v	a	s	t
15	0		75	

$\Rightarrow a = -1.5 \text{ m s}^{-2}$

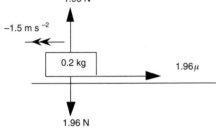

$F = ma$ ∴ $1.96\mu = 0.2 \times 1.5$ ∴ $\mu = 0.153$

22

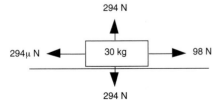

∴ $P = 148 + 207 = 355 \text{ N}$

(Refer to Exercise 8 if you had trouble resolving the weight into 207 N and 444 N.)

23

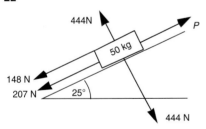

∴ $294\mu = 98$ ∴ $\mu = \frac{1}{3}$

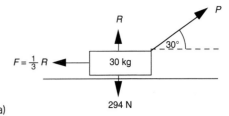

(a)

[Note that F is *against* the motion.]

$(\rightarrow) : P \cos 30° = \frac{1}{3}R$

$(\uparrow) : R + P \sin 30° = 294$

∴ $P = 95 \text{ N (2 s.f.)}$

(b)

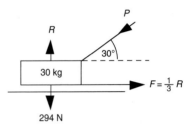

[Note that F is against the motion.]

$(\rightarrow) : P \cos 30° = \frac{1}{3}R$

$(\uparrow) : R = 294 + P \sin 30°$

∴ $P = 140 \text{ N (3 s.f.)}$

24

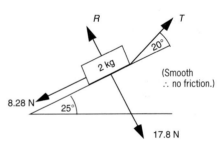

(If need be, refer to Exercise 8 for resolving the weight.)

Up plane: $T \cos 20° = 8.28$

Perpendicular to plane: $R + T \sin 20° = 17.8$

∴ $T = 8.8 \text{ N (1 d.p.)}$

∴ $R = 14.8 \text{ N (1 d.p.)}$

25 $24.5 - T = 2.5a$ $T - 49 = 10a$

∴ $a = -1.96 \text{ m s}^{-2}$ and so the 10 kg mass slides down the plane at 1.96 m s^{-2}.

∴ $T = 29.4 \text{ N}$

26 Again, the 10 kg mass will slide *down* the plane.

$49 - (T + 16.97) = 10a$

$T - 24.5 = 2.5a$ ∴ $a = 0.602 \text{ ms}^{-2}$

27

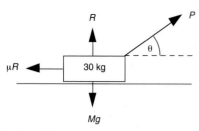

$(\rightarrow):\ P\cos\theta = \mu R$

$(\uparrow):\ R + P\sin\theta = Mg$

Eliminate R and get $P\cos\theta = \mu(Mg - P\sin\theta)$

$\Rightarrow P\cos\theta + \mu P\sin\theta = \mu Mg$

$\Rightarrow P = \dfrac{\mu Mg}{\cos\theta + \mu\sin\theta}$

(An algebraic version of Exercise 23 (a).)

28

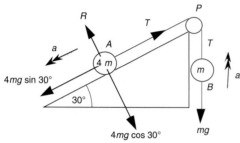

(a) $4mg\sin 30^\circ - T = 4ma$

$\Rightarrow 2mg - T = 4ma$ and $T - mg = ma$

(b) Solve simultaneously to get

$a = \dfrac{1}{5}g$ and $T = 1.2\,mg$

29 (a)

$\tan\theta = \dfrac{7}{24} \Rightarrow$

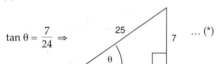

$\dots (*)$

Up plane: $T - Mg\sin\theta - \dfrac{11}{12}R = Ma \quad \dots ①$

Perpendicular to plane: $R = Mg\cos\theta \quad \dots ②$

Hanging mass: $2Mg - T = 2Ma \quad \dots ③$

Substitute for R in ①. Then add to ③

$\therefore 2Mg - Mg\sin\theta - \dfrac{11}{12}Mg\cos\theta = 3Ma$

$\therefore 2Mg - Mg\times\dfrac{7}{25} - \dfrac{11}{12}Mg\times\dfrac{24}{25} = 3Ma$ (from *)

$\therefore a = \dfrac{7}{25}g$, as required.

(b) $\downarrow:$

	u	v	a	s	t
	0	?	$\dfrac{7}{25}g$	0.25	

$\therefore v^2 = 0^2 + 2\times\dfrac{7}{25}g\times 0.25$

$\therefore v = 1.17\ \text{m s}^{-1}$ (2 d.p.)

Section 5

1 (a) $A\ \raisebox{-2pt}{$\curvearrowright$}: 6\times 4 - 7\times 4 = -4\ \text{N m}$

(b) $B\ \raisebox{-2pt}{$\curvearrowright$}: 6\times 4 - 4\times 4 = 8\ \text{N m}$

(c) $O\ \raisebox{-2pt}{$\curvearrowright$}: 3\times 2 - 7\times 2 + 6\times 2 - 4\times 2 = -4\ \text{N m}$

2 (a) $A\ \raisebox{-2pt}{$\curvearrowright$}: 6\times 2 - 8\times 5 = -28\ \text{N m}$

(b) $B\ \raisebox{-2pt}{$\curvearrowright$}: -6\times 3 = -18\ \text{N m}$

3

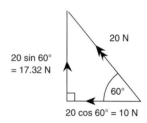

$A\ \raisebox{-2pt}{$\curvearrowleft$}: 17.32\times 10 = 173.2\ \text{N m}$

4 (a) $A\ \raisebox{-2pt}{$\curvearrowleft$}: 9F\times a + 20F\sin 30^\circ\times 3a = 39\,Fa$

(b) $C\ \raisebox{-2pt}{$\curvearrowright$}: 6F\times 3a - 9F\times 2a = 0$

5 In all these questions there is a reaction, R, at the pivot. Therefore it's no good resolving vertically.

(a) pivot $\raisebox{-2pt}{$\curvearrowright$}: 6\times 3 + F\times 3 = 4\times 6 \ \therefore F = 2\ \text{N}$

(b) pivot $\raisebox{-2pt}{$\curvearrowright$}: F\times 6 = 7\times 2 + 5\times 3 \ \therefore F = 4\dfrac{5}{6}\ \text{N}$

(c) pivot $\raisebox{-2pt}{$\curvearrowright$}: 8\times 6 + F\times 4 = 20\times 4 \ \therefore F = 8\ \text{N}$

(d) pivot $\raisebox{-2pt}{$\curvearrowright$}: 8\times 3 = 5\times 1 + 3\times 1 + F\times 4$

$\therefore F = 4\ \text{N}$

6

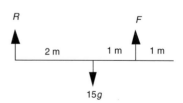

R is force at hinge and F is the supporting force. Once again, it is no good resolving vertically because that gives

$R + F = 15\,g$.

$\therefore$ hinge $\raisebox{-2pt}{$\curvearrowright$}: 15g\times 2 = F\times 3$

$\therefore F = 10g$ or $98\ \text{N}$

$\therefore$ hinge $\raisebox{-2pt}{$\curvearrowright$}: 15g\times 4 + 15g\times 2 = F\times 3$

$\therefore F = 30g$ or $294\ \text{N}$

7

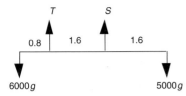

$\uparrow : T + S = 11\,000g$

and $\curvearrowright : T \times 0.8 + S \times 2.4 = 5000g \times 4$

$\therefore S = 68.6$ kN

$\therefore T = 39.2$ kN

8

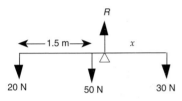

$\uparrow : R = 100$ N

$\curvearrowright :$ right end $: Rx = 50 \times 1.5 + 20 \times 3$

$\therefore x = 1.35$ m

9 (a) $\uparrow : X + Y = 40$

end $\curvearrowright : 0.2X + 0.9Y = 30 \times 0.6$

$\therefore X = 25\frac{5}{7}$ N, $Y = 14\frac{2}{7}$ N

(b)

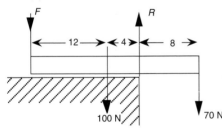

edge $\curvearrowright : 70 \times 8 = 100 \times 4 + F \times 16$

$\therefore F = 10$ N

(c) $\uparrow : 5 \sin 30° + 5 = X \quad \therefore X = 7.5$ N

$\rightarrow : Y = 5 \cos 30° \quad \therefore Y = 4.33$ N

I didn't need to use moments this time.

10 $\uparrow : Y = 4$

$\rightarrow : X + 3 = 5 \quad \therefore X = 2$

corner $\curvearrowright : 5a + Y(a + d) = 0 \quad \therefore d = -2\frac{1}{4}a$

11

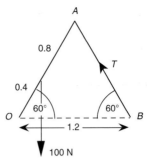

There are forces acting at the hinge O

$\therefore$ we take moments about O.

$O \curvearrowright : 100 \times 0.4 \cos 60° = T \sin 60° \times 1.2$

$\therefore T = 19.2$ N

12 There are forces acting at B

$\therefore$ we take moments about B.

Let force required be F.

$\therefore B \curvearrowright : 200 \times 1.2 = F \times 0.2 \cos 30°$

$\therefore F = 1386$ N

13 $A \curvearrowright : Wa = T \sin 30° \times 2a \quad \therefore T = W$

14

$\uparrow : X + Z = 5 \qquad \qquad \therefore X = \frac{1}{2}$

$\rightarrow : Y = 4 \qquad \qquad Y = 4$

end $\curvearrowright : 5a + Ya = Z2a \qquad Z = 4\frac{1}{2}$

15 (a)

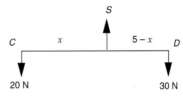

$\uparrow : S = 50$ N

$C \curvearrowright : Sx = 30 \times 5 \qquad \therefore CQ = x = 3$ m

(b) $S = 50$ N

(c)

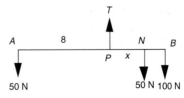

$\uparrow : T = 200$ N

$P \curvearrowright : 50 \times 8 = 50x + 100 \times 3$

$\therefore PN = x = 2$ m

(d) $T = 200$ N

16 (a)

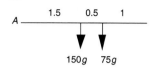

A $\overset{\curvearrowright}{}$: $150g \times 1.5 + 75g \times 2 = 375g$

$\therefore$ 3675 N m

(b) A $\overset{\curvearrowright}{}$: $150g \times 1.5 + 75g \times 3 = 450g$

$\therefore$ 4410 N m

Section 6

1

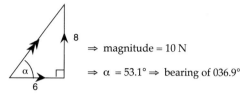

$\Rightarrow$ magnitude = 10 N

$\Rightarrow \alpha = 53.1° \Rightarrow$ bearing of 036.9°

2 $\mathbf{a} = 2\mathbf{i} + 3\mathbf{j} \Rightarrow$ magnitude = 3.6 m s^{-2} (1d.p.)

3 $a - 8 = 0 \Rightarrow a = 8$

4 $b + 10 = 0 \Rightarrow b = -10$

5 $a + 4 = 2a - 6 \Rightarrow a = 10$

6 $5\mathbf{i} + 12\mathbf{j} = 5\mathbf{a} \Rightarrow \mathbf{a} = (\mathbf{i} + 2.4\mathbf{j})$ m s^{-2}

7 $10 + p = 4 \times 8, 4 + q = 4 \times 12 \Rightarrow p = 22, q = 44$

8 (a) $5\mathbf{i} + 8\mathbf{j} = 10\mathbf{a} \Rightarrow \mathbf{a} = (0.5\mathbf{i} + 0.8\mathbf{j})$ m s^{-2}

(b) $-5\mathbf{i}$ N   (c) $-8\mathbf{j}$ N

9 $4\mathbf{i} + 3\mathbf{j}$ has magnitude 5

$\therefore 2(4\mathbf{i} + 3\mathbf{j}) = (8\mathbf{i} + 6\mathbf{j})$ m s^{-2}

10 $-5\mathbf{i} + 12\mathbf{j}$ has magnitude 13

$\therefore 0.5(-5\mathbf{i} + 12\mathbf{j}) = (-2.5\mathbf{i} + 6\mathbf{j})$ m s^{-1}

11 $4(3\mathbf{i} - 4\mathbf{j}) = (12\mathbf{i} - 16\mathbf{j})$ N s

12 $7\mathbf{i} + 24\mathbf{j}$ has magnitude 25

$\therefore 0.5(7\mathbf{i} + 24\mathbf{j}) = (3.5\mathbf{i} + 12\mathbf{j})$ N

13 (a) $10 + b = 3 \times 3, 2 + a = 3 \times 4 \Rightarrow b = -1, a = 10$

(b) $\rightarrow : 20 = U_x + 3 \times 3 \Rightarrow U_x = 11$

$\uparrow : 20 = U_y + 4 \times 3 \Rightarrow U_y = 8$

$\Rightarrow$ initial velocity = $(11\mathbf{i} + 8\mathbf{j})$

14 $\mathbf{a} = 5\mathbf{i} - 2\mathbf{j} \Rightarrow \mathbf{v} = (5t + 4)\mathbf{i} + (-2t + 10)\mathbf{j}$

$\Rightarrow \mathbf{r} = \left(\dfrac{5t^2}{2} + 4t + 1\right)\mathbf{i} + (-t^2 + 10t + 1)\mathbf{j}$

Now $-t^2 + 10t + 1$ is greatest when the derivative = 0

$\therefore -2t + 10 = 0 \Rightarrow t = 5$

$\Rightarrow$ maximum $y = -25 + 50 + 1 = 26$

15 Momentum = $4(3\mathbf{i} + 4\mathbf{j}) = 12\mathbf{i} + 16\mathbf{j}$ N s

16 (a) $2(1.5\mathbf{i} + 8\mathbf{j}) + 5(-2\mathbf{i} + 8\mathbf{j}) = 7\mathbf{V}$

$\Rightarrow \mathbf{V} = (-\mathbf{i} + 8\mathbf{j})$ m s^{-1}

(b) $2(-\mathbf{i} + 8\mathbf{j}) - 2(1.5\mathbf{i} + 8\mathbf{j}) = -5\mathbf{i}$ N s

17 (a) Momentum after =
$50(250\mathbf{i} + 50\mathbf{j}) + 40(100\mathbf{i} + 200\mathbf{j})$

$= 16\,500\mathbf{i} + 10\,500\mathbf{j}$.

This is different from the momentum before of $90(200\mathbf{i} + 100\mathbf{j})$

$\therefore$ It cannot be an internal explosion.

(b) $90(200\mathbf{i} + 100\mathbf{j}) + 15V = 16500\mathbf{i} + 10500\mathbf{j}$

$\Rightarrow V = (-100\mathbf{i} + 100\mathbf{j})$m s^{-1}

18 $\mathbf{a} = 2\mathbf{i} - \mathbf{j}, \mathbf{v} = 2t\mathbf{i} - t\mathbf{j}, \mathbf{r} = (t^2 + 3)\mathbf{i} + (-\dfrac{t^2}{2} + 1)\mathbf{j}$

19 $\mathbf{a} = \mathbf{i} - 3\mathbf{j}, \mathbf{v} = (t + 1)\mathbf{i} + (-3t - 1)\mathbf{j}$

$\Rightarrow \mathbf{r} = \left(\dfrac{t^2}{2} + t + 1\right)\mathbf{i} + \left(-\dfrac{3t^2}{2} - t + 1\right)\mathbf{j}$

20 $m\mathbf{a} = 3\mathbf{i} + 3t\mathbf{j} \Rightarrow m\mathbf{v} = 3t\mathbf{i} + \dfrac{3t^2}{2}\mathbf{j}$

$\therefore$ $t = 5 \Rightarrow$ momentum $= (15\mathbf{i} + 37.5\mathbf{j})$ N s

21 $t = 0, \mathbf{r} = -3\mathbf{i} + 12\mathbf{j}$; $t = 1, \mathbf{r} = 8\mathbf{j}$

$t = 2, \mathbf{r} = 3\mathbf{i} + 4\mathbf{j}$; $t = 3, \mathbf{r} = 6\mathbf{i}$

$t = 4, \mathbf{r} = 9\mathbf{i} - 4\mathbf{j}$.

(a) The path is shown in the following diagram.

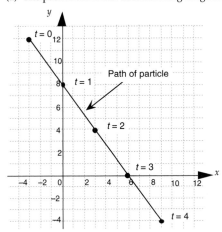

(b) The particle is closest to the origin when the magnitude of:

$\mathbf{r} = (3t - 3)\mathbf{i} + (12 - 4t)\mathbf{j}$ is least.

This is equivalent to finding the minimum value of:

$(3t - 3)^2 + (12 - 4t)^2$

Simplify the brackets to get $25t^2 - 114t + 153$

Now complete the square to get $(5t - 11.4)^2 + 23.04$

$\therefore$ Least value occurs when $5t - 11.4 = 0$

$\therefore$ when $t = 2.28$.

(c) Looking at the diagram, this certainly seems reasonable – the particle is closest somewhere between $t = 2$ and $t = 3$.

The least value will be $\sqrt{23.04} = 4.8$ cm

(Alternatively you could drop a perpendicular from the origin to the line $3y + 4x = 24$, solve simultaneously and get $x = 3.84, y = 2.88$. Then substitute back and get $t = 2.28$)

An important example: give it some thought.

22 $(5\mathbf{i} + 4\mathbf{j})$ m s^{-1}

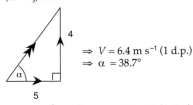

$\Rightarrow V = 6.4$ m s^{-1} (1 d.p.)
$\Rightarrow \alpha = 38.7°$

$\therefore$ 6.4 m s^{-1} on a bearing of 051.3° (1 d.p.)

23 $3\mathbf{i} - (\mathbf{i} + 6\mathbf{j}) = (2\mathbf{i} - 6\mathbf{j})$ m s^{-1}

24 (a) $(t - 2)\mathbf{i} + (3t - 1)\mathbf{j}$

(b) $(t - 2)^2 + (3t - 1)^2 = 10t^2 - 10t + 5$

Complete the square to get $10(t - \tfrac{1}{2})^2 + 2\tfrac{1}{2}$

$\therefore$ $t = \dfrac{1}{2}$ for the least value.

(c) This least value $= \sqrt{2\tfrac{1}{2}} = 1.58$ m (2 d.p.)

25 After the collison both particles must have direction $16\mathbf{i} - 12\mathbf{j}$.

But $16\mathbf{i} - 12\mathbf{j} \Rightarrow$

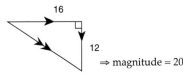

$\Rightarrow$ magnitude $= 20$

$\therefore$ a **unit vector** in the direction of motion will be $\dfrac{1}{20}(16\mathbf{i} - 12\mathbf{j}) = 0.8\mathbf{i} - 0.6\mathbf{j}$.

(A **unit** vector is a vector whose magnitude is one.)

(a) $0.8\mathbf{i} - 0.6\mathbf{j}$

(b) $0.2(16\mathbf{i} - 12\mathbf{j}) = 0.2\mathbf{V} + 0.3 \times 10(0.8\mathbf{i} - 0.6\mathbf{j})$, where $\mathbf{V}$ is velocity vector of A after collision (the conservation of momentum equation).

$\therefore$ $\mathbf{V} = (4\mathbf{i} - 3\mathbf{j})$ m s^{-1}, velocity of A

and $(8\mathbf{i} - 6\mathbf{j})$ m s^{-1}, velocity of B

(c) Impulse $= 0.2(4\mathbf{i} - 3\mathbf{j}) - 0.2(16\mathbf{i} - 12\mathbf{j})$
$= (-2.4\mathbf{i} + 1.8\mathbf{j})$ N s

26 (a) At time t: position vector of $Q = 2\sqrt{3}\mathbf{i} + \mathbf{v}t$

and position vector of $P = 2\mathbf{j} + 3\mathbf{j}t$

They collide at time T

$\therefore$ $2\sqrt{3}\mathbf{i} + \mathbf{v}T = 2\mathbf{j} + 3T\mathbf{j}$

$\therefore$ $T(\mathbf{v} - 3\mathbf{j}) = 2\mathbf{j} - 2\sqrt{3}\mathbf{i}$

But the velocity of Q relative to $P = \mathbf{v} - 3\mathbf{j}$

which equals $\dfrac{1}{T}(2\mathbf{j} - 2\sqrt{3}\mathbf{i})$

$\therefore$ $\mathbf{v} - 3\mathbf{j}$ has the direction $2\mathbf{j} - 2\sqrt{3}\mathbf{i}$

(b) $\mathbf{v} - 3\mathbf{j} = \dfrac{1}{T}(2\mathbf{j} - 2\sqrt{3}\mathbf{i})$

$\Rightarrow \mathbf{v} = -\dfrac{2}{T}\sqrt{3}\mathbf{i} + \left(\dfrac{2}{T} + 3\right)\mathbf{j}$ $\therefore k = \dfrac{2}{T}$

(c) $\mathbf{v} = -k\sqrt{3}\mathbf{i} + (k + 3)\mathbf{j}$ has magnitude $3\sqrt{3}$

$\therefore$ $3k^2 + (k + 3)^2 = 27$

$\therefore$ $k = 1.5$ or -3 (quadratic)

But $k > 0$ $\therefore$ $k = 1.5$

(d) $T = \dfrac{2}{k} = 1\dfrac{1}{3}$